"You will identify with Leigh █████████████████ and inspirational moments from ███████████████ feel like you've made a new friend, as she leads you into the greatest of all relationships."

ED YOUNG
senior pastor, Second Baptist Church,
Houston, Texas

"Singles lead productive, purposeful lives but are at times mingled with pain and loneliness. Leigh McLeroy ably guides us to the durable peace that lies on the far side of pain. Her unflinching honesty results in God-centered insights rich in wit and wisdom, grace and hope. This book is her gift to us all."

GLENN LUCKE
president, Docent Communications Group;
coauthor, Common Grounds

New Life Live! Meditations

MOMENTS FOR

SINGLES

LEIGH MCLEROY

introduction by STEPHEN ARTERBURN

NAVPRESS®

BRINGING TRUTH TO LIFE

OUR GUARANTEE TO YOU

We believe so strongly in the message of our books that we are making this quality guarantee to you. If for any reason you are disappointed with the content of this book, return the title page to us with your name and address and we will refund to you the list price of the book. To help us serve you better, please briefly describe why you were disappointed. Mail your refund request to: NavPress, P.O. Box 35002, Colorado Springs, CO 80935.

The Navigators is an international Christian organization. Our mission is to reach, disciple, and equip people to know Christ and to make Him known through successive generations. We envision multitudes of diverse people in the United States and every other nation who have a passionate love for Christ, live a lifestyle of sharing Christ's love, and multiply spiritual laborers among those without Christ.

NavPress is the publishing ministry of The Navigators. NavPress publications help believers learn biblical truth and apply what they learn to their lives and ministries. Our mission is to stimulate spiritual formation among our readers.

Published in association with the literary agency of Alive Communications, Inc. 7680 Goddard Street, Suite 200, Colorado Springs, Colorado, 80920.

NAVPRESS, BRINGING TRUTH TO LIFE, and the NAVPRESS logo are registered trademarks of NavPress. Absence of ® in connection with marks of NavPress or other parties does not indicate an absence of registration of those marks.

ISBN 1-57683-540-5

Cover design by David Carlson Design
Cover image by Caroline Woodham/PhotoDisc
Creative Team: Dan Rich, Steve Halliday, Darla Hightower, Glynese Northam

Some of the anecdotal illustrations in this book are true to life and are included with the permission of the persons involved. All other illustrations are composites of real situations, and any resemblance to people living or dead is coincidental.

Unless otherwise identified, all Scripture quotations in this publication are taken from the *New American Standard Bible* (NASB), © The Lockman Foundation 1960, 1962, 1963, 1968, 1971, 1972, 1973, 1975, 1977, 1995. Other versions used include: *THE MESSAGE* (MSG). Copyright © 1993, 1994, 1995, 1996, 2000, 2001, 2002. Used by permission of NavPress Publishing Group; HOLY BIBLE: NEW INTERNATIONAL VERSION® (NIV®). Copyright © 1973, 1978, 1984 by International Bible Society. Used by permission of Zondervan Publishing House. All rights reserved; the *Contemporary English Version* (CEV) © 1995 by American Bible Society. Used by permission; the *New King James Version* (NKJV). Copyright © 1982 by Thomas Nelson, Inc. Used by permission. All rights reserved.; and the *King James Version* (KJV).

McLeroy, Leigh
  Moments for singles / Leigh McLeroy ; introduction by Stephen Arterburn.-- 1st ed.
    p. cm. -- (New life live meditations)
  ISBN 1-57683-540-5
  1. Single people--Prayer-books and devotions--English. I. Title. II. Series.
  BV4596.S5M335 2004
  242'.64--dc22

                                        2003024024

Printed in the United States of America

1 2 3 4 5 6 7 8 9 10 / 08 07 06 05 04

FOR A FREE CATALOG OF
NAVPRESS BOOKS & BIBLE STUDIES,
CALL 1-800-366-7788 (USA)
OR 1-416-499-4615 (CANADA)

In memory of
Victor, Jane, and Charlie.
You lived it. I'll see you when I get home.

Contents

INTRODUCTION

My marriage ended after twenty-one years. The struggles we had over the years were never a secret. I have written and spoken openly about them for some time. But it was a devastating blow that struck me to the core of all that I am.

Full of grief and sorrow I moved on with my life, some days having to tell myself to breathe and other days reminding myself to look somewhere other than down at my feet. I was scared and alone and I did not know where to turn except to the friends who have always been there for me. Fearing public humiliation was my plight, I felt my career and calling were over and I would never write again. But that was not to be the case. Slowly I began to crawl toward the end of the darkest tunnel of my life. There was no light at the end, but I knew there was an end. Some days it was just God and me. On other days I was surrounded by the love and support of my extended family and friends who seemed to have just been waiting for me to reach out to them at a time when they were so needed. If you ever face what I faced, I pray that you will be as fortunate to have people around you to love you.

Of course there are many more who do not come to the single life the way I did. You may have always been single and wonder if you always will be single. No matter how you arrived at your single position, I want to share with you what I have learned about it in the short time I have returned to it. These are not earth-shattering truths but they are life-giving realities. First, I discovered you must trust God with your future. It must be a seeking of God's kingdom first, not when and if you find someone who loves you. It must be God for God's sake, not for the sake of a partner. No bargaining with God for what you will give up to be granted a mate. You must live with the intention that even if you remain single all your life, you will remain faithful to God.

Secondly, you must turn to friends or develop them. We were not meant to be in isolation. We were meant for community. God's community. And no matter how difficult connection has become for you, it is the key to the single life. You must connect in community and live your life as if it will always be your life, rather than waiting for someone to bring you to life someday. God has an adventure for all of us and it is best we get on with living out the adventure and purpose God has chosen for us.

Additionally, every single person needs direction and encouragement through God's Word and wise direction. That is what this book is meant to bring you. Long before it was published I had access to the wisdom, comfort, encouragement, and challenges that are between these covers. I hope you find them as rich and meaningful as I have.

Finally, let me leave my thoughts here with one word of caution. There are books that I have read through quickly, gotten the gist of, and moved on. I want to encourage you to not let this be one of them. Take your time. Read this slowly as if spending time reading these words was spending time with God and worshiping him. Let the words have time to seep into your soul and then reflect on them throughout the day. If you do, I think you will turn the last page more satisfied, more fulfilled and more motivated to find and live the life that God has chosen for you. There are some great moments waiting for you, I hope you take your time and experience them to the fullest.

Stephen Arterburn is host of the radio program, New Life Live. He is also the founder of Women of Faith conferences, the author of more than fifty books and the recipient of two Gold Medallions for writing excellence. He and his daughter reside in Laguna Beach, California. He can be reached at Sarterburn@newlife.com.

Belonging

Living single in a doubles' world

Our hunger for connection is God-created, and it is good.
The yearning to connect with others in an intimate and personal
way is part of our design, and it is no mistake.
What is a mistake is to believe that marriage is the
primary answer to our desire to belong.

ARE YOU ALONE?

The lights had not yet gone out when I chose my seat: midway up and near the center of the row. Fewer than a dozen people had scattered in twos and threes around a stadium-style theater that easily seated two hundred, but no one sat on the row I selected. It had been a hard day at work, and a darkened theater, a tall Diet Coke, and a mindless movie seemed like the ideal way to unwind.

It almost was.

Out of the corner of my eye I saw him come in. He scanned the room as if he might be looking for a friend, then headed straight for "my" row. He didn't sit on the end, either. He came within one seat of me and plopped down noisily. When the lights dimmed and the previews began, he put his arm on the armrest of the seat in between us and leaned in.

"Are you alone?" he whispered.

I looked his way in the dark and he spoke again. "Are you waiting for someone?"

I took my drink, my coat, and my purse and silently stumbled out the other end of the row. In a shaking voice I asked the theater manager to refund my unused ticket, and drove home feeling more frustrated, more rattled, and more vulnerable than when I'd walked in.

That's because the answers to the stranger's questions were yes, and yes.

Yes, I was alone. Even more disconcerting, it showed. And yes, I was waiting for someone — *am* waiting for someone — have *been* waiting quite a long time for someone. Not just to sit next to me for an afternoon movie, but to stay beside me for life.

In that, I am, statistically speaking, not alone at all.

Fifty years ago, about one in ten households could be designated "single-person." Today that ratio is closer to one in three. Adults are marrying less, marrying later, and divorcing more often (and earlier) than ever before. From 1970 to 2000, the proportion of never-married men and women ages 30-34 more than tripled. Even by age 44, 15 percent of adults have never said, "I do." Baby boomers today are 500 percent more likely than their parents to be single by choice, chance, or divorce.

Even so, ours is still very much a couples' world.

Wedding and party invitations to singles are often addressed "and guest," as if to come alone would be unthinkable. Cruises and travel packages cost more for single travelers who desire their own accommodations. Married couples may hesitate to include their single friends when planning time with other married folks — or worse — count on them to babysit! Those singles confident and secure enough to dine solo in a nice restaurant do not often get rewarded for their self-assurance by receiving the best table in the house.

Those of us who "do life" alone have become accustomed to a myriad of everyday reminders that "couples rule." These reminders feel more annoying than hurtful. But underneath them lies the uneasy feeling that — no matter what the statistics tell us — if we wear no wedding band, we don't quite *belong*.

God, it's just me. Have You noticed? As much as I try not to, sometimes I feel like one half of a really great pair of shoes. I have so many good things in my life that it seems ungrateful to keep asking You for this one thing, but where else would I take my request? I want to share my life with someone. And I want any choice that brings me joy to bring You glory. Wanting only one or the other would make my life considerably less complicated, but I still want them both. I know that You are completely aware of my situation, and that You have plans for my welfare — plans to give me a future and a hope. Even knowing that, I don't always rest easily. So please remind me often that I am Yours, and that I am not alone. I'll never stop needing to hear that, no matter what my future holds.

WHO WOULD YOU CALL?

In the days after September 11, I felt mesmerized by reports of conversations between those victims who knew all was lost and the men and women who loved them. Scores of the doomed pressed their cell phones into service and dialed a husband or a wife for the final time. They spoke hurried words they hoped would somehow convey a lifetime of feeling. They said things like "I love you so much" or "Please be strong" or "Tell the kids I'll be watching over them," and then they said goodbye.

As I read these heartbreaking reports, I couldn't help but wonder: *Who would I have called?* My dad, who shares coffee with me almost every Friday morning at a mid-town diner? Or my mother, the member of my immediate family most reachable by phone at any given hour? Or perhaps my sister, my best friend since childhood and my truest confidant today? I'm not sure.

And that's the point. There is no *one* person whose name would (and should) rise to the top of my list. It's not that there isn't *anyone;* it's that there is no *one* in particular. I have never made a promise to leave my father and mother and cleave to another until death should part us.

A common denominator among the single — whether never married, divorced, or widowed — is a nagging uncertainty about where we fit in. In between our family of origin (or our former spouse) and our hoped-for future, yawns a vast, open expanse of unmapped relational landscape with no road signs that say, "Here. This is your place."

We've spent our share of solitary weekends and attended more than our quota of weddings. (I personally have enough bridesmaid dresses to allow an entire class of third-grade girls to play dress-up without sharing.) We've endured the queries of relatives and well-meaning friends who ask, "Are you seeing anyone?" and been secretly disappointed when they *stopped* asking. We've eaten our share of holiday dinners at the "children's" table. And many of us have done it just long enough to buy into the belief that everyone with a spouse magically "belongs."

But that's not necessarily so.

The happiest, most satisfied men and women I know are not defined by the presence or absence of a mate, but by their relationship with their Maker. Conversely, the most miserable people I know are those who — married or single — continue to look to another person for their identity.

Our hunger for connection is God-created, and it is good. The yearning to connect with others in an intimate and personal way is part of our design, and it is no mistake. What *is* a mistake is to believe that marriage is the primary answer to our desire to belong. Marriage certainly offers a consistent setting for love to be regularly exercised and demonstrated, but marriage itself doesn't "create" love or give lovers their identity.

Only God does that.

*Long before he laid down the earth's foundations, he had
us in mind, had settled on us as the focus of his love, to be
made whole and holy by his love. Long, long ago he
decided to adopt us into his family through Jesus Christ.
(What pleasure he took in planning this!) He wanted us
to enter into the celebration of his lavish gift-giving by
the hand of his beloved Son. . . .*

*It's in Christ that we find out who we are
and what we're living for.*

(EPHESIANS 1, MSG)

THE JOY OF FIRST LOVE

Do you remember your first love? I remember mine. His name was Michael, and I believed with all my sixteen-year-old heart that he was the eighteen-year-old answer to my prayers. I anticipated his phone calls each night and fell asleep remembering the sweet sound of his voice. I counted the hours until we could see one another again and must have driven my parents crazy for the six roller-coaster months that we dated. I adored Michael...but Michael didn't stay. (In retrospect, I can see that this was a good thing. A *very* good thing.)

Michael's love delighted me, but it was not the permanent kind. And as much as I enjoyed being the object of his affection some twenty-plus years ago, I never think of myself today as Michael's former girlfriend — or anyone else's former girlfriend. The love that defines me is much bigger than that.

I am the object of God's desire and He went to great lengths to make me His. St. Augustine said, "God loves each of us as if there were only one of us." Very early in life it became undeniably clear to me that God Himself loved me. For reasons that I could not then and cannot now explain, He chose me to be His beloved. His love for me was, and still is, over the top — and better yet, He is not going anywhere!

While I usually name Michael as my first love, that's not wholly true. My first love is the One who "first loved" me, the One who has kept on loving me through every other love of my life:

> *In this is love, not that we loved God, but that He loved us*
> *and sent His Son to be the propitiation for our sins. We love,*
> *because He first loved us. (1 John 4:10,19)*

Receiving the love of God does not mean that I renounce my desire to be married. It means that I feel secure in knowing that I am deeply loved today — right now! — and that, even single, *I belong*. I don't need to frantically search for a mate to validate me or impart to me status or identity. And because I am certain that God loves me in Christ, I can more gracefully and unselfishly love those He brings into my life — without regard to whether they qualify as potential "marriage material." I can love them as real people with real needs, real gifts, and real longings of their own.

Feeling secure in God's "first love" for me makes me less likely to expect from marriage more than God ever meant it to give. Loved by Him, I am freer than I might otherwise be to see marriage as what Martin Luther called it on the eve of his unexpected wedding to Katherine Von Bora: one of the gifts of God "to be taken on the wing."[1]

God, words cannot express the security that comes from knowing that You loved me first and will always love me best. Whether I am ever someone else's mate, I am Yours forever. Your love will make me a better lover of others than I could ever hope to be, left to my own miserable devices. Knowing I have been perfectly loved gives me hope that I can love in ways that mirror Your love for me.

Thanks for Michael, God. That was sweet. And thanks for the other wonderful men you have brought into my life. They don't tempt me to love You less. They inspire me to keep on loving You more and more.

THE BENEFITS OF BEING SINGLE

The single among us can easily cite what we see as the obvious benefits of marriage: shared responsibility, companionship, freedom of sexual expression, children, and the opportunity for emotional intimacy. We often find pointing to what we *don't* have much easier than appreciating what we do have.

Believe it or not, married people do this too! Even the happily married may remember their time before marriage as unencumbered, independent, and adventurous, and occasionally long for the more uncomplicated existence of being "one" and not "two."

If you are single (and probably you are if you are reading this), you really *do* have advantages. Take pleasure in what you have, even as you continue to hope for a mate. Your present satisfaction does not cancel out your desire, and your desire does not prevent your present satisfaction. Hope for marriage should never result in losing your delight in living.

Sadly, some singles reason like this: *I must not appear happy or satisfied, even for a moment, or God will think I'm fine as I am and not bring me the mate I desire.* We're like toddlers who think we must cry nonstop to get the things our parents know we need. Never let your appetite for a future mate destroy your capacity for real-time joy.

Instead, ponder your advantages:

- You have more control over your discretionary time.
- You are free to serve God in a multitude of ways.
- You may give yourself to a greater number of relationships, without the need to consistently prioritize any one.
- You may live and work anywhere you please.
- You have more flexibility to change your plans at a moment's notice, often without worrying about how someone else might be impacted by your decision.
- You have fewer distractions that might keep you from pursuing a deeper relationship with God.

As you consider these advantages, consider also these promises that God has made to His own:
- Eye has not seen, nor ear heard, nor have entered into the heart of man the things which God has prepared for those who love Him. (1 Corinthians 2:9, NKJV)
- I will be a Father to you, and you shall be My sons and daughters, says the LORD Almighty. (2 Corinthians 6:18, NKJV)
- Be of good courage, and He shall strengthen your heart, all you who hope in the LORD. (Psalm 31:24, NKJV)
- For the Father Himself loves you, because you have loved Me, and have believed that I came forth from God. (John 16:27, NKJV)
- Be anxious for nothing, but in everything by prayer and supplication, with thanksgiving, let your requests be made known to God; and the peace of God, which surpasses all understanding, will guard your hearts and your minds through Christ Jesus. (Philippians 4:6-7, NKJV)

You *belong*. You are loved by God. He has made it possible for you to join His family, a family that sin and death can never destroy.

If you long for marriage, long for marriage. It is a good and honorable thing to desire. But don't expect that finding a mate will provide your life with meaning and purpose. It won't. It wasn't meant to.

God already has done that.

For we are God's workmanship, created in
Christ Jesus to do good works, which God prepared
in advance for us to do.

(EPHESIANS 2:10, NIV)

FORGIVENESS

MAKING PEACE WITH THE PAST

God feels no surprise at your sin or mine. He knew
what an enormous price our redemption
required, and He planned accordingly.
His Son's sacrifice was ample. It is ample.

FORGIVING OTHERS

Listen to three of the costliest words in the English language: "I forgive you."

Forgiveness is never a freebie; someone always pays. Tim Keller, pastor of Redeemer Presbyterian Church in Manhattan, says that every wrong done creates a debt that someone must pay, in one way or another. Just think about it: You slight a friend, the words get repeated, and a rift ensues. The slighted friend feels wounded and you feel embarrassed. Either you will pay or he will. Either you will go to your friend and ask forgiveness, thus paying the debt, or your friend will slowly extract payment by returning your slight with whispered words of his own or coolness toward you or outwardly expressed anger. But until forgiveness gets offered and received, the debt remains.

Each of us has a catalog of wounds we've received in the regular course of day-to-day living. No one is immune. These hurts come by accident, as a consequence of our own actions, or by someone else's careless hand. They may be the result of betrayal, spite, or envy; or they may seem to have no reason at all behind them.

"The hurt that creates a crisis of forgiving has three dimensions," wrote theologian Lewis Smedes. "It is always personal, unfair and deep. When you feel this kind of three-dimensional pain, you have a wound that can be healed only by forgiving the one who wounded you."[2]

Even as I write these words, I confess that I have "open accounts" not yet resolved — and I know from listening to the stories of others that I am not alone.

Maybe you're still reeling from a divorce you never wanted or a subversive power play that left you jobless. Or perhaps you suffered abuse at the hand of a family member or a friend, or were abandoned by a parent when you most needed his or her love and support. Maybe a close friend betrayed you, or you contracted a disease you never expected, or you were cheated by a business associate you trusted to do the right thing. I don't have to list all the possibilities; you can surely fill in the blanks without assistance.

Our sins not only alienate us from one another, they create a deep divide within our own hearts. And sometimes that divide makes it impossible for us to connect with others in a loving way, no matter how much we may long for it. For those of us who are unmarried, the old, unresolved wounds can actually prevent us from opening ourselves to the love we desire — and even cause us to pretend we're "relationship ready" when we're not.

If you can't seem to get past the hurts of your past — either the ones you've received or those you've inflicted — you may need help in sorting things out. Consider seeking out a trusted friend, a pastor, or a counselor to ask for guidance in the process of healing and forgiveness. Admit that you haven't been able to do it alone, and receive a fresh perspective on what might be a very old and nasty wound. I have found that when I want to experience change and release more than I want to nurse my pain, forgiveness becomes possible and healing can begin.

"Forgive us our debts," I have prayed so often, "as we forgive our debtors." Only I don't always forgive my debtors, God. So I'm asking You to do something that I have failed to do more than once, and I'm hoping in Your goodness that You will. I'm also asking You to prick my heart with the conviction that I am a forgiveness-debtor myself and need to seek the forgiveness of others I have hurt, either knowingly or by neglect. Help me to want restored relationships more than I want to be right or self-righteous. Thank You for Your Son, who has made a way for my sins to be forgiven and my relationship with You to be completely restored. That's a debt I'll never be able to repay — and one that You've sworn to remember no more.

FORGIVING YOURSELF

The single person seated across from me was a hostage. His captor? Himself.

He had been given an opportunity for servant leadership in his church and he was carefully and quietly explaining to me why he couldn't accept it. Why he didn't deserve it. The situation involved an indiscretion in his past. Yes, he'd sought forgiveness from the persons he had wronged. Yes, he'd asked for God's forgiveness and believed he had received it.

He just couldn't seem to forgive himself.

As I listened to him, my heart ached. He obviously expected me to agree that his secret sin disqualified him from service. But I couldn't and I didn't. Even so, nothing I could say changed his outlook. I saw in his eyes that my words about the grace of the crucified Christ didn't budge his resolve. He hadn't finished crucifying himself.

Not only have I seen others in this man's situation — I've been in his shoes. I've insisted on sitting as judge and jury over my own offense and delivered my own sentence, even when grace would have freed me. (I'll bet you have too.) Oh, I've confessed. I've asked for forgiveness from those I've wounded. I've laid my sin before God. But plenty of times I have refused to leave it there. Instead, I've decided that my mistakes were too awful to be excused and determined to do more than God required of me. To "pay extra" — as if I could add a thing to the price He's already paid for my ugly, shameful sin.

I asked Jesus Christ to be my savior when I was just a child. The pastor of our church came to our home, sat in the living room with my parents and me, and explained the gospel in simple terms a child could understand. To me, his visit amounted to an afterthought. I'd done the deal already in my heart. But when he finished talking, he asked me if I had any questions at all about what I'd heard. Only one came to mind: "Does this cover every bad thing I've done so far, or everything I'll ever do?" I laugh now when I think of it, but in truth, I knew I had a lot more potential for sin than actual practice at it. He knew it too, and he smiled when he said, "Everything, period."

God feels no surprise at your sin or mine. He doesn't draw the line at abortion or abandonment or dishonesty or promiscuity and say, "I can forgive anything but *that*." He knew what an enormous price our redemption would require, and He planned accordingly. His Son's sacrifice was ample. It *is* ample.

> *If we walk in the Light as He Himself is in the Light, we have fellowship with one another, and the blood of Jesus His Son cleanses us from all sin. If we say that we have no sin, we are deceiving ourselves and the truth is not in us. If we confess our sins, He is faithful and righteous to forgive us our sins and to cleanse us from all unrighteousness. (1 John 1:7-9)*

Because of His Son's sacrificial death, God already has agreed to forgive those who will repent, *period*. He forgives child abusers who ask for His mercy. Liars, drug dealers, and prostitutes do not get turned away from the throne of grace. Deceivers, thieves, and drunks are candidates for His redeeming touch — and so am I. God's heart is *that* big. His mercy is *that* deep. His forgiveness is *that* rich.

Now, what was that wretched sin you've been holding over your own head? Do you think, in light of what He's already done, that you might allow His grace to cover you and let yourself go free?

———

Do not be deceived; neither fornicators, nor idolaters,
nor adulterers, nor effeminate, nor homosexuals, nor
thieves, nor the covetous, nor drunkards, nor revilers,
nor swindlers, will inherit the kingdom of God. Such
were some of you; but you were washed, but you were
sanctified, but you were justified in the name of the Lord
Jesus Christ and in the Spirit of our God.

(1 CORINTHIANS 6:9-11)

THE ONE WHO *DOESN'T* NEED FORGIVING

We need forgiveness. And certainly we need to forgive others. But there is One who never needs forgiveness: God Himself. He has never erred and His ways are beyond reproach.

Even when they baffle us.

Even when they seem unfair.

Some of us haven't dealt with our God-grudges, and it's about time we did.

If we believe that God is sovereign — that He has absolute sway over the events of our lives — then we will surely struggle when those events feel unsettling or frightening or confusing or sad. Those of us who profess belief in God must, at times, admit an uncomfortable clash between our faith and our feelings. And we singles who want to be married must come to terms with the fact that God's sovereignty extends over even our love lives.

Several years ago I heard a young woman give an amazing testimony. She quite openly spoke of her past; the details were not pretty. She had been very promiscuous, and after several abortions, a dancing gig in a men's club, and a string of broken relationships, she came to church. There, she met people who accepted her. Eventually she came to know Jesus and experience His love and forgiveness. Not long after her conversion, she met a fine Christian man and the couple got engaged. Her joy seemed electric. People applauded her story and praised God's goodness to her.

I applauded too. Then I thought, *That's great for her, God — but what about me? I've been here at church for a long time; she only just arrived. Now about that husband You're giving her . . . do You think You could work on mine?*

If I believe that God is the Giver of every good and perfect gift (and I do), how do I deal with how He's not given me some of the gifts I've most longed for? Although my heart has its own spots, my past looks comparatively good — yet I'm still waiting for what this woman already has received.

I know my situation pales when I consider parents who have lost their children, or those who have suffered unspeakable abuse or neglect, or even those who have become martyrs for the cause of Christ. I'm certainly not in their league, nor have I experienced anything like the suffering of Job. But I confess there are times in the deep of night that I question God's attentiveness to me or wonder why He's chosen thus far to withhold what seems like an ordinary blessing. I don't blame Him; I can't.

But I have questioned His ways.

Lewis Smedes wrote:

> *We do hate God sometimes. All of us, I think. On the sly. If we dare not hate the Giver, we do dare hate his gifts. When we shut our eyes to every reason we have for being glad to be alive, when we resent good things that happen to our friends, when our hearts stifle every happy impulse, we are nurturing a passive hatred of God.[3]*

What grudge are you holding against Him? For what perceived neglect does your heart secretly condemn Him? What slight do you accuse Him of when no one else can hear?

Careful! His ways lie beyond your judgment or mine.

Our Lord never deserts us and He Himself can never disappoint us. But our expectations of Him sometimes lead us to deep dissatisfaction. When Jesus began to speak hard truth to His disciples, they hesitated. They felt confused by talk of His coming death and resurrection and put off by His claims that no one could come to Him unless the Father granted it. His actions didn't match their expectations — and many of them began to desert Him.

"You do not want to go away also, do you?" Jesus asked the twelve men closest to Him.

"Lord, to whom shall we go?" asked Simon Peter. "You have words of eternal life. We have believed and come to know that You are the Holy One of God" (John 6:67-69).

"When God gets us alone through suffering, heartbreak, temptation, disappointment, sickness, or by thwarted desires," wrote Oswald Chambers, "when He gets us absolutely alone, and we are totally speechless, unable even to ask one question, then He begins to teach us."[4]

We may feel disappointed in what God has (or hasn't) done. But the bottom line for us remains the same as it was for Peter: To whom else shall we go? There is no one else. He is beyond questioning. Life exists nowhere else. He alone is the One who satisfies us, even in our unmet longings.

So tell Him the truth about how you feel. Confess your weakness. Proclaim His sovereignty.

Then follow Him all the way home.

O my God, I cry by day, but You do not answer; and by night, but I have no rest. Yet You are holy, O You who are enthroned upon the praises of Israel. In You our fathers trusted; they trusted and You delivered them. To You they cried out and were delivered; in You they trusted and were not disappointed.

(PSALM 22:2-5)

Healing

Living beyond loss

Even if its fruit is lovely, hardly anyone welcomes loss.
Each of us, if we could, would choose a kinder tutor.
But some gifts come with the death of a thing
that can be gotten in no other way.

Healing a Broken Heart

Breaking up is hard to do. It's hard the first time, and it never seems to get easier. Even a mutual decision to part ways with someone you've loved can produce an awful ache. Those who've endured the pain of divorce sometimes argue that death might hurt less. (Widows and widowers would certainly dispute that.) Sorting through the jumble of emotions that a loss of love can bring feels painful, no matter how that loss occurred.

As anyone with experience knows, the demise of a relationship is no "one hurt per party" proposition. Hearts break in hundreds of ways, and seldom all at once. Grieving comes in waves, but with no predictable rhythm. Its tides defy scheduling; its undertows can feel downright mean.

Jumping into another relationship while your blood still pours out from the last one may seem like a quick fix, but it is never a wise solution. Neither is pulling the covers over your head and hiding until you feel like rejoining the living. (It could be quite some time before you "feel" like it.)

So what might help?

No one can say for certain what will bring you comfort, but here I offer some things that have comforted me. Consider this a kind of cafeteria line for the wounded. Choose whatever looks good to you; take as much or as little as you like.

Go ahead and *catalog your losses.* Seriously. Write down everything you believe you've lost, real or imagined. You'll make the list in your mind anyway; you might as well commit it to paper. Maybe you've lost your best friend. Say so. Or perhaps you've lost the children you never had but only dreamed of. Or someone who could finish the crossword puzzles you could only start. Or the laugh you liked better than any other laugh in the world. Exhaust the possibilities — then read your list over, maybe even out loud or to a trusted friend.

Thank God for everything you listed. If you'd never had it, you couldn't have counted it as loss. Each thing you named was a gift — and the source of all gifts is certain: "Every good thing given and every perfect gift is from above, coming down from the Father of lights, with whom there is no variation or shifting shadow" (James 1:17). Thank Him for the good things He has given you, however fleeting.

Forget about forgetting. You probably won't, and you shouldn't. Every experience, every delight, every heartbreak become part of your own unique story. Resist the temptation to try and wipe the slate clean. Instead of erasing your past, invite God to use it: "Blessed be the God and Father of our Lord Jesus Christ, the Father of mercies and God of all comfort, who comforts us in all our affliction so that we will be able to comfort those who are in any affliction with the comfort with which we ourselves are comforted by God" (2 Corinthians 1:3-4). Nothing — not even a love that didn't last — is wasted by our God.

Tell God how you feel. C. S. Lewis once advised a friend to pray as he was, not as he thought he ought to be. False bravado does not fool God. If your heart is broken, say it's broken. If you feel hopeless, confess your hopelessness. If you are angry, admit your anger. King David told God, "I am poured out like water, and all my bones are out of joint; my heart is like wax; it is melted within me" (Psalm 22:14). David never wasted any time trying to disguise his feelings!

Allow other loves in. This world offers many kinds of love. *Eros,* or romantic love, is hardly the only variety. Don't push every love aside because you've lost one love. Remember to receive the kindness of *phileo,* or friendship love. Welcome the presence of a concerned friend who comes alongside to comfort, with or without words. Allow others in your life to care for you for a little while. (You'll surely return the favor.)

Wait. The place you live now is not where you will always be. The psalmist wrote, "Weeping may endure for a night, but joy cometh in the morning" (Psalm 30:5, KJV). Mother Teresa said that the worst misfortune this life can bring, from the perspective of eternity, will seem like one night in a bad hotel. Surely with His help and one another's, we can endure *that.*

He heals the brokenhearted and binds up their wounds.
He counts the number of the stars; He gives names to all
of them. Great is our Lord and abundant in strength;
His understanding is infinite.

(PSALM 147:3-5)

NEVER AGAIN!

It's over. Friends and family have been "notified." Phone calls and e-mails have ceased. Personal property has been divided or returned. Mutual friends have been consulted and any future plans together cancelled. It's a done deal. You've ended a relationship, either willingly or with some measure of regret. If you are like most people, at some point in the near future you will utter words similar to these: "I will *never* love someone again. It just hurts too much. I don't have the courage/strength/endurance/desire to try again. Never."

The words feel right at the time, and others surely understand. They may not even call you on it . . . for a while, anyway. Depending on the degree of trauma involved, your friends will allow you a "grace period" for regaining your perspective. They'll disregard any threats to leave the country, quit your job, change churches, or enter a convent. They'll avoid saying your ex's name aloud in your presence, and refrain from discussing their own relationships with the opposite sex in a positive light. *For a while.*

The last time I said "never again" I was sitting with my sister in the bakery of a grocery store at 6:30 A.M., red-eyed and nursing a bad cup of coffee. (Family members are more likely to appreciate the tremendous self-control involved in waiting until sunrise to call for emergency counseling.) After she heard me out, offering tissues and plenty of empathy, she said these profound words (especially considering the hour): "Leigh, if you're lucky, it's going to work out only *one time*."

My sister says that I'm the one whose words have left her speechless since childhood, but on that day, it was me who had nothing more to say. She was right. Once is all it takes. But the odds of an "only" love becoming that "always" love on the first try are very, very slight indeed. Hardly anyone escapes heartbreak on the way to happily ever after, if there even *is* such a thing as happily ever after.

The truth is, failure in romantic relationships happens more often than success. Failure in relationships sometimes *leads* to success. And here's a funny thing: I've never met a happily married person who said, "I can't tell you how deeply I regret every failed relationship I had before I met my spouse. None of it was worth it. I didn't learn a thing. I wish I'd quit after the first time I experienced failure." Hasn't happened once.

Saying "never again" doesn't ensure an unbroken heart, but it may eventually ensure an unbreakable one. C. S. Lewis said,

> Love anything and your heart will be wrung and possibly broken. If you want to make sure of keeping it intact you must give it to no one. . . . Lock it up safe in the casket or coffin of your selfishness. But in that casket, safe, dark, motionless, airless, it will change. It will not be broken; it will become unbreakable, impenetrable, irredeemable. To love is to be vulnerable.[5]

Maybe the scariest word in relationships is not the "c-word" (commitment), but the "v-word" (vulnerability). And maybe the worst thing that can happen is not that we might fail at love, but that we might make good on our vow to never try again.

———————————

God, help me to never say "never again" when it comes to loving. Whether it's a friend, a child, a new love, or an old one, teach me that the one thing worse than opening my heart and being vulnerable is refusing to and becoming cold.

A phrase in John's gospel inspires me to keep on loving. Jesus is about to eat the Passover for the last time with the handful of friends closest to Him. He knows He's destined for death, and He knows who will desert Him in His darkest hour. "Jesus, knowing that His hour had come . . . having loved His own who were in the world, He loved them to the end" (John 13:1).

Give me the courage to love like that!

THE RING GAME

The "ring game" goes something like this: A single person at a party, a church, a wedding, or even on a trip to the mall, looks at the left hand of almost every adult he or she sees. Is there a wedding ring? If there is, what does the ring-wearer have that you do not? Is he or she more attractive? Better dressed? More confident? Friendlier? What obvious advantage does this married person have that you, the unmarried ring-checker, lack?

When I catch myself playing the ring game, I know it's time for a little self-examination. If I'm busy looking for reasons why married people are married, I'm probably trying to explain why I am not. I find that I play the ring game most often when a relationship in which I have invested deeply has ended. I imagine that if I can change something about myself that seems substandard, I may "qualify" for the blessing of marriage.

This game has plenty of flaws, some of them obvious and some so subtle that I need God's help to see them for the pitiful lies that they are.

Lie #1: *You must be perfect (or considerably better than you are right now) to be married.*

A new nose, a better paying job, or an extra set of reps at the gym is *not* the ticket to coupledom. All the married have flaws too, because *everyone* is flawed, period.

Lie #2: *Marriage is a merit badge for spiritual maturity.*

How many times has some well-meaning someone said, "When you finally give it all to God, He will bring you a mate"? No one on this side of heaven "finally" gives it all to God. The Bible says that when we see Him, we shall be like Him; but until then, we are in the slow process of being *transformed* into His image (see 2 Corinthians 3:18).

Lie #3: *Your standards are too high.*

The subtext here is that anyone who truly desires to be married will be able to find someone who'll marry them. And that may be right. But imagine living the rest of your life with a stunt double for the man or woman who kept his or her standards high while waiting for you.

Lie #4: *There is no one left worth having.*

You're left, aren't you? Are you no one? Marriage is not like grade school kickball. You know, the last one chosen is the least desirable player. Charles Spurgeon said, "The longer the blessing is in coming, the richer it will be when it arrives. The blessing which costs us the most prayer will be worth the most."[6] Prayerful longing is a sure and steady investment in tomorrow. Despair nets nothing but more despair.

Lie #5: *You're being punished.*

In other words, you would be married (or remarried) by now if not for (fill in the blank with your own heinous sin). Of all the ring-checker lies, this one is the worst. First, it assumes that God is not a God of grace; second, it assumes that those who are married deserve the good thing they've been given. Both assumptions are dead wrong.

At the root of each of these ugly fallacies sits one great lie: God gives us what we deserve and withholds from us what we do not deserve. But in Christ, God has withheld what we deserve — punishment by death for our sins — and at great cost, given us what we do not deserve — the forgiveness of our trespasses according to the riches of His grace.

Remember this the next time you feel compelled to play the ring game. And if you find that you still want to play, then at least opt for a different version. Put your own name in Haggai 2:23 (NIV) and try on a different kind of ring:

"On that day," declares the LORD Almighty, "I will take you, my servant _____," declares the LORD, "and I will make you like my signet ring, for I have chosen you," declares the LORD Almighty.

God, forgive me when I play the ring game and get caught up in thinking it's all about me. It's not and I know it. For so many years I believed marriage was a given. A right. I know now that it is so much more than that. If I marry, it will not be because I've earned it as a reward, but because You have given it to me as the thing it always was, whether I knew it or not: a gift that reflects Your goodness, not mine.

LOSING TO GAIN

Remember Peter Pan? Almost everyone does, thanks to books, bedtime stories, and Walt Disney's classic animation.

Peter is the forever young, green-tights-and-gherkin clad boy from Neverland who refuses to grow up — and his fantastical adventures with Tinker Bell and the Darling children have woven their way into our cultural consciousness.

Lots of folks remember Peter, but fewer seem familiar with his creator, Scotsman James Matthew Barrie. Fewer still can point to the circumstances that likely caused the Edinburgh-educated Barrie to pen his beloved children's story nearly one hundred years ago.

Barrie wrote of "lost boys" because he knew of lost boys. The seventh of ten children, he suffered the death of his older brother David (said to be his mother's favorite) when he was just a child. David's death made him forever a boy to his grieving family. Then when Barrie himself became an adult, he befriended Arthur and Sylvia Llewelyn Davies — the parents of five boys — and adopted all five of them after their parents' untimely deaths. *Peter Pan* grew from the stories he spun for the orphaned Davies boys, no doubt inspired by the memories of his own lost sibling.

Yet even if it bears lovely fruit, hardly anyone welcomes loss. Each of us, if we could, would choose a kinder tutor. But some gifts come with the death of a thing that can be gotten in no other way.

The loss of a relationship is a kind of death. When it happens, it feels like nothing good could possibly result from it, either now or in the future. Thankfully, we can rely on something stronger than our feelings. Jesus taught His disciples to rely on this in preparation for His own death. He taught them the principle of losing to gain.

> *"Listen carefully: Unless a grain of wheat is buried in the ground, dead to the world, it is never any more than a grain of wheat. But if it is buried, it sprouts and reproduces itself many times over. In the same way, anyone who holds on to life just as it is destroys that life. But if you let it go, reckless in your love, you'll have it forever, real and eternal." (John 12:20-24, MSG)*

Just days after Jesus spoke these words, His followers felt sure that the very worst thing that could happen, had. Jesus died as a criminal on a Roman cross, and their hopes and dreams of a future with Jesus as their friend and king died along with Him. But when it looked as though all had been lost, Jesus proved His teaching true by appearing to them again, risen from the dead! His resurrection changed everything — and not only for them, but also for us.

So what does that have to do with your loss, your grief, your present heartache? Just this: Now that a kind of death has come, begin to look for the signs of life sure to follow. J. M. Barrie's loss brought the world the magic of *Peter Pan*. Surely without the tragedy he experienced, it would never have been born. Jesus' death brought the miracle of resurrection, and because it did, it's reasonable that we should look for "little resurrections" everywhere.

Is your heart broken? Does all seem lost? Take your sorrow to the One who has defeated death and offer it to Him as a gift. Then watch, hope, and pray. A seed has been planted that will — on a day you least expect — sprout new and green in a tiny glimpse of resurrection glory. I can't say how. No one can. But I can say for certain that the story of your loss is not over yet.

Not by a long shot.

Now may the God of hope fill you with all joy and peace
in believing, so that you will abound in hope by the
power of the Holy Spirit.

(Romans 15:13)

HOPE

STAYING POSITIVELY EXPECTANT

*Hope requires humility and bravery — two character traits
that seldom comfortably coexist. It takes humility to
admit that there's something quite ordinary that you
have not managed to "get" for yourself.
It takes bravery to keep believing that one day soon,
it might be given to you as a gift.*

HOLDING FAST TO HOPE

Leave it to the news magazines to offer my dreams an editorially assisted suicide.

Some people's hopes get derailed in a hospital room or a board-room or a courtroom; mine have been challenged more than once in the grocery store checkout line. It was there I learned I was more likely to be killed by a terrorist than married after forty (news that came, thankfully, before I reached that milestone). And then another blow: "Babies vs. career: the harsh facts about fertility."

It seems, according to a *Time* magazine piece, that only 0.1 per-cent of babies born in the U.S. are born to women age forty-five and older; and that at age forty-two, 90 percent of a woman's eggs are abnormal, and she has only a 7.8 percent chance of giving birth without scientific intervention. So what about those Hollywood moms who are having perfectly beautiful babies well into middle age? Donor eggs, *Time* tactlessly revealed.

I always wanted four children. For as long as I can remember, I dreamed of having two sons and two daughters, spaced evenly through my prime childbearing years, like brightly colored dividers in a clean, new notebook. A nice plan — except I didn't marry young. Somewhere around twenty-seven, I began mentally moving the dividers closer to each other. Later I would learn that twenty-seven is precisely the age at which a woman's chance of getting pregnant begins to decline. (Was my body sending my heart a message when I adjusted my expectations at just that age?) It seems, too, that nature self-selects when we don't police our bodies on our own: at twenty, the risk of miscarriage is about 9 percent; it doubles by age thirty-five, and then doubles again by the time a woman reaches forty.

I've done the math. Should God in His goodness bring a husband tomorrow, and should I beat the odds and conceive almost immediately, even then I'd be on the wrong side of the rough in nine months' time. Hope is getting harder and harder to nurture — but it hasn't disappeared altogether.

I've noticed that friends and family don't speak of children as a given for me anymore. No one says casually in conversation, "You'll see when you have kids of your own." Even so, I'm often thrust into the inevitable kid-conversations that spring up among women my age. If they do happen to realize that I'm the odd one out, they offer comments that sound polite, but don't hurt any less. "You must have so much free time," they say, or "At least your living room isn't ankle deep in toys." It's not. But I've never seen that as the enviable consolation prize for childlessness.

As strange as it may sound, in my completely unwilling failure to reproduce, I don't feel less feminine or less complete. Each passing year finds me feeling more nurturing, deeper, wiser, fuller, and more free. And a strange paradox has arisen: While the likelihood that I will give birth dwindles, the hope that I will give life grows stronger by the day.

I realize I'm not the only one whose dreams have been seriously delayed. I know there are far worse things than being without a husband and children. But this is *my* desire, so it's the only one from which I can authoritatively speak. I know others who had the very things I long for, then saw them wrenched away by tragedy or self-ishness or simple neglect. I know that some pray for cancer to vanish, or still limbs to stretch and move, or the hardened heart of another to melt, or to hear that they're finally forgiven. My heart goes out to them. I want them to keep hoping too.

But for God, I would give up. It's more than a little embarrassing to remain in a helpless and hopeful posture for this long. But because I know Him, I hold fast to hope. I've simply seen too much to do anything else, despite what the headlines say.

God, help me to look expectantly to the future that, even now, You are forging for me. Help me to believe that Your good lovingkindness is for me, and not just for others. Help me to count on You, to hope in You with confident assurance. Please! It's midnight, and I'm here — begging for my bread before the only One who can give it. Prepare a banquet for me, just because You are good. Please God . . . will You do that for me?

ONE BRIGHT RED BIRD

I'd gone to the country for a few days of quiet. I needed to be fortified — not just to catch up on lost sleep, but to experience the kind of soul rest that can elude me in my normal routine. I felt beat, and I wanted to stay in a place where I could privately lick my wounds and listen for God with no distractions.

I visited a house both small and sparely furnished. I've grown to love its sitting room with a soot-marked stone fireplace, a high, wood ceiling, and a tiny loft tucked underneath its beams. The simple kitchen holds one small table, four chairs, and a cushioned window seat. A double bed with a chenille coverlet makes a bridge between the two rooms.

The house's furnishings feel comfortable and calming, but they are not fine. Two gently-worn arm chairs and an ottoman face the fireplace, and an antique Bible lies open on the table beneath the window. A long church pew stretches across the back wall, and on it I piled my bag, blanket, and books — all that I brought with me to this solitary place.

Late into the night, with a fire crackling and a steaming cup of tea in hand, I wrote these words: *How is it possible to long for something so deeply and never see it? Haven't I trusted in You, God, or have I only not trusted in me? Is the desire of my heart from You, and if so, haven't You promised to give it if I delight myself in You? Have I failed to do that? Then when? How? I have waited on You alone. I want this gift to come from You. I have no 'plan B.' Did Sarah ever remind You of her age, God? This Saturday is my birthday, and You know which one. My desire is the same as it's ever been. All my distractions and old allegiances are gone. Killed. Severed. I am no one's now but Yours. I need You to do for me what I cannot do for myself. You are my only hope.*

The next morning, just after sunrise, I sat at the kitchen table, looking out at the woods, stark and bare in late December. The trees had long since shed their leaves, and everything looked gray and faded like an old photograph. The view lacked even a single color — until one bright red bird fluttered in and perched on a distant limb.

He looked more than obvious. He was outrageous! Even his beak flamed red. He stood out with no effort on his part; he couldn't help but be seen. My eyes stayed riveted to him, willing him to stay and not fly off with the only glimpse of color in a landscape devoid of contrast. And he did stay. As I watched him, I thought of the little red-coated girl in *Schindler's List.* His appearance seemed that vivid. That strange.

My outlook still felt bleak. My dreams continued to hide out of sight. But into this frame fluttered one bright red bird, like a brilliant deposit of faith — and he looked so beautiful I could not look away. His bold color seemed almost as ridiculous as the hope of a forty-year-old woman for a family of her own. But he was there — and he flew!

I don't know much, but I am certain of this: The God who made the cardinal red and slipped him into my sight line that winter morning is the very One to whom my hope should fly. He is my strength, my song, and my salvation — and the Giver of every good thing.

Therefore, brethren, since we have confidence to enter the holy place by the blood of Jesus, by a new and living way which He inaugurated for us through the veil, that is, His flesh, and since we have a great priest over the house of God, let us draw near with a sincere heart in full assurance of faith, having our hearts sprinkled clean from an evil conscience and our bodies washed with pure water. Let us hold fast the confession of our hope without wavering, for He who promised is faithful.

(HEBREWS 10:19-23)

EXPECTING GOOD THINGS

He caught me!

Sitting at a stoplight at a busy intersection, I had just checked myself out in the rearview mirror: licked my teeth, pursed my lips together to more evenly smooth my lipstick, and given my hair a quick fluff. With the last motion, the man in the car next to me smiled broadly, gave me the "okay" sign, and mouthed the words, "You look perfect." Feeling slightly ridiculous and delighted at the same time, I mouthed back, "Thanks a lot," and prayed for the light to quickly change.

But I smiled all the way to dinner.

I don't expect reassurance from a total stranger at rush hour. Still, being on the receiving end of an enthusiastic thumbs-up felt nice, even for just a few seconds. (I should probably add that he stared out from a tinted window, which almost certainly worked in my favor!) And whether he was a hopeless flirt, or just an attractive, thirty-something guy who felt benevolent on a Friday afternoon, I'm glad God put him in the lane next to me and caused him to look my way. His encouragement made me hopeful.

For me, one of the hardest things about being single is wondering if there's something not-quite right that has caused me to be passed over or rejected in favor of a more attractive, more worthy prospect. And along with that, the fear that I may always be alone. It's sometimes easier to resign myself to the prospect of lifelong singleness than it is to hope. Hope requires humility and bravery — two character traits that seldom comfortably coexist. It takes humility to admit that there's something quite ordinary that you have not managed to "get" for yourself. It takes bravery to keep believing that one day soon, it might be given to you as a gift.

Since childhood, I've practiced *not* saying what I most want. I wanted a horse for years, but I (mostly) kept quiet about it. I was a city girl and felt fortunate to have a dog. I didn't want to press my luck. I wanted to be editor of my high school yearbook, but my best friend got chosen instead. I said I didn't mind. I did. I've been a bridesmaid many times and said "yes" gladly. I would rather have died than admit that each time felt bittersweet because I didn't *want* the role of understudy. I wanted to be a bride. But I never said so. Pride keeps me from any open display of longing — and most people I know are the same.

If pride keeps us quiet about our longings, cowardice keeps us from nurturing them. We fear being disappointed, so we abandon hope. We may believe good things await others, but refuse to hope for them ourselves.

For the Christian, the thing gets even more complicated. If I say I believe in God and am trusting Him to supply my needs, then if He doesn't "come through," will my open hope damage His reputation? (I wonder when we pray, "Thy will be done," if we are less concerned with our own submission and God's glory than we are about the consequences of our own misdirected shame and fear.)

The truth is, if God needs my protection, He's not big enough to worship. But He doesn't, and He is.

Where do we get the humility and courage that we need to hope? I believe it comes through faith. If we belong to God in Christ, we're His heirs and He wants to glorify Himself through the big and small things in our lives. We're not slaves. We're sons and daughters. If we've trusted Him for salvation, isn't it right and reasonable to trust Him for everything? Paul thought so: "What then shall we say to these things? If God is for us, who is against us? He who did not spare His own Son, but delivered Him over for us all, how will He not also with Him freely give us all things?" (Romans 8:31-32).

If I trust Him with my hope, God will be glorified by it. I will not be put to shame; nor will He. Whether He satisfies my hope with marriage or with something that I can't yet see, He *will* satisfy it. I can expect good things from Him, because He is a very good God.

For You are my hope; O Lord GOD, You are my confidence from my youth. By You I have been sustained from my birth. . . . My praise is continually of You.

(PSALM 71:5-6)

PURPOSE

REDEEMING THE DAYS

*God is the least fooled of anyone when we pretend to be pleased
with another day or week or year of being single —
and we are not. He couldn't possibly be honored when we
offer thanks for a thing for which we are not only not thankful,
but secretly resentful. But I believe He actually welcomes
an honest question like, "Why did You give me
this God? What is Your purpose in it?"*

THE BEST LAID PLANS

In his hugely successful *7 Habits of Highly Effective People,* management guru Stephen Covey coaches his readers to "begin with the end in mind." That's good, common sense advice. No matter what the undertaking, it's best to have a mental picture of where you're headed. For a long time, my mental picture was of a wedding. I had an end in mind of me in an elegant white dress, walking down the center aisle of the church on my father's arm, ready to be handed off at the altar to the man of my dreams.

Then what? Well, for a long time, I didn't give much thought to what might come after that imagined moment, other than the children I also hoped for. I don't think I believed I would get married then die soon afterward, but I certainly didn't have much of a firm goal for my life beyond marriage and a family and doing a bit of writing.

Then a funny thing happened to the end I had in mind. It didn't come when I thought it would. In fact, that particular "end" has yet to come! I've had to rethink my life's purpose, rather than assume the default to be marriage. Nine out of ten women eventually do marry, so the odds remain in my favor. But marriage is no longer my life's purpose. If it were, I'd have been in prep school about as long as Moses herded his father-in-law's goats in Midian.

Author and theologian Frederick Buechner has suggested that God calls us to the place where our great joy and the world's great hunger meet. In other words, God has placed desires and longings in my heart that respond to some very real needs in His world. Purpose involves discovering my God-intended reason for being, and structuring my life to that end. That means seeking a goal for my life that goes beyond the question of who I might spend it with!

Purpose is a large and weighty thing, so I've found that it helps to think in broader terms, and then refine. Broadly speaking, every Christ-follower has a similar purpose. The Westminster Shorter Catechism asks, "What is the chief end of man?" and provides this still-relevant answer: "To glorify God and enjoy Him forever." Paradoxically, the way for me to know my own purpose is to first take the focus off myself. Apart from God, I am hopelessly self-absorbed and self-oriented; I will never fulfill my purpose outside of His good and guiding presence.

Once I settle the central issue of whom I will glorify and enjoy, I am free to explore those gifts, desires, and passions God has placed in my heart. This discovery is a process, not a documented program. Consider a few questions that might help you uncover these God-planted things, if you have not done so already:

- What keeps you up at night? What kinds of things can you do in which you completely and delightfully lose track of all time?
- In what activities or pursuits can you expend energy and not feel depleted, but energized?
- What do others consistently see and praise in you? (This is not to say your calling is whatever someone else decides it is, but often others see gifts in us that we remain unsure of.)

- What makes you weep or clench your fists? Does some injustice or hurt call forth tears from you, either in sadness or in frustration?
- If the necessary resources were available to you, what passion or opportunity would you most want to pursue?
- If you had to answer the question "Who are you?" with one word, what would that one word be? Are you a healer? A leader? A writer? A teacher? A nurturer? A truth teller? Listen to your heart.

British writer Dorothy Sayers said that work is not what we do to live, but what we live to do, the thing that gives us mental, spiritual, and physical satisfaction, and the means by which we offer ourselves to God.

Have you decided yet how you will offer yourself—and for whom?

For I know the plans that I have for you,
declares the LORD, plans for welfare and not for
calamity to give you a future and a hope.

(JEREMIAH 29:11)

SINGLE ON PURPOSE

You may not be single by choice. But have you considered being single "on purpose"?

Most of my single friends would like to be married. A few say they could be content to remain single for life; even fewer claim to have the gift of singleness. On the contrary, under the right circumstances, almost every single adult I know would choose the gift of marriage. But by definition, a gift is something chosen for us, not something we choose.

If God has chosen for you — today — the gift of singleness, will you gratefully receive it? Will I? And beyond receiving it, will we actively seek His design, not just for our lives in general, but for our present, unmarried state?

When my sister and I were young, she had an unusual way of receiving gifts she didn't particularly like. I admired it, actually. While I would dutifully smile at the odd-gift giver and (insincerely) say, "Thank you very much," Lynn would eye the unwanted gift, look at the giver, and say, "What did you give me *this* for?" (It drove my mother crazy.)

Looking back, I think my sis was on to something. God is the least fooled of anyone when we pretend to be pleased with another day or week or year of being single — and we are not. He couldn't possibly be honored when we offer thanks for a thing for which we are not only *not* thankful, but secretly resentful. But I believe He actually welcomes an honest question like, "Why did You give me *this*, God? What is Your purpose in it?"

Are you honest enough (and brave enough) to ask God what His purposes might be for your singleness?

Is it such a stretch to think He might use your longing, your struggle, your hurt (or mine) to show His glory and advance His cause? In her beautiful book, *Holding on to Hope*, Nancy Guthrie writes of her submission to God's purpose in losing two infant children to a rare genetic disorder. "For me, submission has meant a quiet, though sorrowful, acceptance of God's plan and God's timing. But because I believe God's plans for me are better than what I could plan for myself, rather than run away from the path he has set before me, I want to run toward it."[7] Her honesty humbles me. There is no denying that her words have been refined in the fire of experience and are spoken in trusting love.

A few years back one of my single friends gave me the following words, which we both posted on our screensavers at work: "Were there any place better for you than the one in which you find yourself, Divine Love would have placed you there." Although she is now married and has a small daughter — and I am still single — it's hard to argue with that thought. If this is, in fact, the best place for me, I want to seize and celebrate it, and not miss whatever purpose God might have in placing me here.

Don't you want the same thing?

God, I didn't choose this, and I won't pretend I did. I
never thought I'd be alone, and certainly not for this
long. Looking back, I can see that great good has come
from my single life. Thank You for travel and teaching
and time carved out to go where I've felt called and
needed. Thank You for the precious, crazy quilt of
friends I've made and the memorable things we've shared
together. Thank You for one gloriously illuminating trip
to Brazil, for another sad and bittersweet one to
Canada, and for the life lessons I learned in both places.
Thanks for the times when it was only You and me, and
for what those focused hours have yielded. Show me
what to say "yes" to tomorrow, and the day after, and the
day after that. Let me be single on purpose, and let that
purpose be Yours.

THE WAITING PLACE

A few years ago I recorded a snippet of Dr. Seuss's *Oh, the Places You'll Go* on my home answering machine. It was a clever bit about "the waiting place ... where everyone is just waiting. For a train to go or a bus to come, or a plane to go or the mail to come ... or a phone to ring or the snow to snow ... just ... waiting."[8] I liked it a lot.

But after hearing it for the first time or two, friends began to complain. Hardly anyone enjoyed sitting through "the waiting place" to leave their message.

No surprise. We don't, most of us, enjoy waiting at all. It very quickly loses its dubious charm. But I know few people who are not, at any given time, waiting for *something*. Many of us are waiting (openly or secretly) for marriage. Others are waiting to receive test results or to reach the front of the checkout line. To welcome home a loved one. To hear their name called on a try-out list. To be asked to dinner or to dance. To see a stoplight or a season change. To hold a baby in their arms.

Like it or not, we all do our time in the waiting place. The question is, what are we *doing* with the time? Do we simply languish, or are we willing to linger and learn while we wait? My answering machine message lasted too long to avoid annoyance, but not long enough to multitask. Most of our wait-times, however, can be put to good use.

In *My Utmost for His Highest,* teacher Oswald Chambers writes, "There are not three levels of spiritual life — worship, waiting and work. Yet some of us seem to jump like spiritual frogs from worship to waiting, and from waiting to work. God's idea is that the three should go together as one."[9]

The Bible is full of wait-ers to keep us in good company. Sarai. Elizabeth. Hannah. Moses. David. Hosea. Jonah. Job. What might we have heard if their inner voices had been recorded?

It's no use. I'll never have a child. Or, *Why shouldn't I be stuck with someone else's sheep for the rest of my life? I'm a murderer. I'm no good for anything else.* Or, *Samuel must have mistakenly anointed me. Saul will kill me before he ever lets me become king.*

Some wait-ers languished in self-doubt and pity — for a while. But more often than not, these God-followers learned to linger in their waiting places and see what there was to see. And usually what there was to see provided strong evidence of a great, provident God at work — in the smallest of circumstances and in the hidden places of the human heart.

Some things only God can do. We should wait on Him to do them. But others we can and should do, even as we wait on God. Only He can change a heart, redeem a life, and engineer the circumstances that can put us in the path of another at just the right time. But we can and should be faithful to those tasks already at hand: nurturing our spiritual growth, serving others, discovering our gifts, becoming emotionally healthy, keeping physically fit, and being good stewards of our finances. This work is ours.

A wise friend once told me that we are never alone in the cold, dim cave of uncertainty. When our eyes adjust to the half-light, we see that there are tens, hundreds, thousands even, waiting right along with us. And maybe, he said, waiting for a word *from* us that injects hope or humor or sense into a time that seems to make no sense at all.

So here is a word of encouragement from me to you: Good things can and will happen, even as we wait.

———————

Do you not know? Have you not heard? The Everlasting God, the LORD, *the Creator of the ends of the earth does not become weary or tired. His understanding is inscrutable. He gives strength to the weary, and to him who lacks might He increases power . . . those who wait for the* LORD *will gain new strength.*

(ISAIAH 40:28-29,31)

WE INTERRUPT THIS PROGRAM . . .

When did someone last ask you, "What are you doing?" and you unapologetically answered, "Nothing"?

Most of us fill our date books, calendars, and PDAs with to-do lists and appointments that overwhelm our waking hours. I admit I love the feeling of crossing completed items off my own agenda and that my sense of accomplishment feels heightened on those days when I manage to burn through an entire list. But activity can be a shabby idol, and serving it does not guarantee satisfaction. I know. I've tried.

When my friends and I commiserate about how busy we are, I wonder if we're not trying to convince one another (and ourselves) how much we "count" in the grand scheme of things. And I wonder, too, what would happen if we slowed down and thoroughly sifted our calendars until only the weightiest priorities remained.

A dear friend once told me that she suspected when she got to heaven, she would not be asked how many nutritionally balanced meals she served, how many Bible classes she taught, how many carpool miles she drove, or how many diapers she changed. "What I think I'll be accountable for," she said, "is how well I loved."

Funny thing about love: It's mostly penciled-in on the fly.

A quick read of the Gospels confirms that Jesus' time was in great demand, but He never over-scheduled Himself. He remained both purposeful and flexible. He moved resolutely toward Jerusalem — toward His own sacrificial death — but not necessarily in a straight line. He allowed interruptions. Sick people interrupted His journeying. His own disciples interrupted His sleep. Children interrupted His teaching, and although His disciples felt annoyed, He did not. He allowed His Father to direct Him, moment by moment.

God has every right to interrupt my life too. My time is not my own; it's His. And His agenda should take precedence over mine every time.

As a single person, I may get confused about this and lapse into believing that I am the keeper of my days, that productivity somehow trumps love. It does not. God has the right to "interrupt my program" as He sees fit, and I must learn not only to allow those interruptions, but also to welcome them. The truth is, most of the uncrossed items on my list can wait. But what He is calling me to do in the moment may be a one-time opportunity to love, custom-made just for me.

And I'll discover it only by saying yes.

———————

God, I confess that I use busy-ness both to protect myself
from feeling useless, and to deflect those things I fear or
dread. I can even use it to keep from thinking too much
about things that hurt, or from hearing Your own still,

small voice. Even as I make my list and set my schedule, keep me mindful of the fact that every moment is Yours. You have the right to shake up my day in whatever way seems right to You. If Your own Son never got too busy to pencil in love for those who needed it, how can I refuse Your ad hoc assignments? Make me more sensitive to others, God. Teach me to ask, "What would You have me do?" and obey the answer You give.

In this life there will always be bills to pay, groceries to buy, laundry to do, and dogs to walk. There will always be budgets and meetings and presentations and deadlines. But when time is no more, it will only be You, and Yours. Until then, interrupt me for either — anytime.

PERMISSION

LIVING LIFE IN THE "NOW"

*If we singles really imitated Jesus — if we really gave
ourselves permission to serve —
I believe the world would be changed.*

PERMISSION TO GROW

I distinctly remember selecting my china and silver patterns — and in retrospect, I waited far too long to do so. I was nearly thirty and had been using handed-down odds and ends for years, waiting for a marriage proposal to give me permission to start making a home. Instead of wandering around a department store with a barcode scanner and a doting fiancé, I simply took one plate and one piece of silver to the counter and asked the clerk for two place settings of each. (She thought I was buying wedding presents for friends!)

I realize that dishes aren't a big deal, but deciding to join the grown-up world and make responsible solo choices is. Today I can quite confidently furnish my home, organize an elegant dinner party, or plan and execute a trip to a foreign country. I'm comfortable with career challenges and changes and I'm not afraid to negotiate or take the lead when the situation calls for it. I pay my own bills and have not built up a massive debt to present to some unsuspecting man as an unwelcome dowry-in-reverse.

Even though it's natural to see marriage as a rite of adult passage, it's not reasonable to refuse to grow up just because you're single. Or single again. And while certain things (plumbing problems, car salesmen, maps, or anything mathematical) can render me pretty helpless, I'm not going to refuse to join the functioning adult world because I happen to be unmarried.

It's not just the details of life that some of us singles put off handling. Sometimes we get stuck emotionally, socially, and spiritually too. But married or single, God's goal for us is maturity.

> *As a result, we are no longer to be children, tossed here and there by waves and carried about by every wind of doctrine, by the trickery of men, by craftiness in deceitful scheming; but speaking the truth in love, we are to grow up in all aspects into Him who is the head, even Christ, from whom the whole body, being fitted and held together by what every joint supplies, according to the proper working of each individual part, causes the growth of the body for the building up of itself in love. (Ephesians 4:14-16)*

God has specially gifted each of us who belongs to Him, and He means for us to use those gifts — regardless of our marital status. I was going to fully exercise my gifts of writing and teaching when I could retire from my nine-to-five career and focus on my family and ministry. But if I had stubbornly refused to alter that self-made plan, I'd still be waiting to do both.

If I had decided to wait until I was married to entertain friends or travel or invest myself in the lives of children, I would be a very shallow, very immature person indeed! And if I had determined to wait for a husband to feed and lead me spiritually, I'd still be a baby in the things of faith.

A precious friend of mine died at the age of ninety-one, never having married. "Miss Jane" called herself an "unclaimed blessing" with a twinkle in her eye. She never took herself too seriously, even in her last years, but oh, she was serious about following Jesus! She taught the Bible for more than seventy years. She served her church faithfully and never looked back. I never saw Jane that she did not kiss me on the cheek, even if it was the third time she'd seen me in one day! She was the most alive, most vibrant, most winsome woman — and although she was born in an era when a woman's life was defined by her marital status, Jane's was not. She kept growing until the day she died — and she encouraged others to do the same.

I used to look at Jane and think, *Oh, God, don't let me become like her*. Now I remember her and implore Him to do just that — to make me a beautiful, loving woman who's stretched out in pursuit of the life He's planned just for me.

For it is for this we labor and strive, because we have fixed our hope on the living God, who is the Savior of all men, especially of believers. . . . Let no one look down on your youthfulness, but rather in speech, conduct, love, faith and purity, show yourself an example of those who believe.

(I TIMOTHY 4:10-12)

PERMISSION TO GRIEVE

Although it was late, I didn't feel sleepy. As I flipped through cable channels with the remote, I paused on an interview with former *Today Show* weatherman Willard Scott. It wasn't Willard *per se* that caused me to stop, or his interviewer, CNBC's Tim Russert. It was the painful catch I heard in Scott's voice. He sounded as if he were about to cry.

Willard Scott is a showman, a funny man, someone more associated with laughter than tears. As I listened to him speak of his wife of forty-seven years, Mary, and her death from breast cancer less than a year before, Willard Scott did cry. But his voice carried an undercurrent of joy and tenderness, even through his tears. Then he looked at Russert and said, "You know, she was crazy about you."

Forget *The Bachelor* or *Survivor. That's* reality television.

Real life is not scripted. It doesn't have a predetermined end. And it gets plenty messy sometimes. Willard Scott gave himself permission to grieve during his CNBC interview, and it wasn't hokey or phony. It was touching and true.

Have you given yourself permission to grieve the pains and losses of your life? Or are you trying to cover them up and soldier bravely on?

I love the biblical story of Naomi, a widow who leaves her homeland of Jerusalem with a husband and two sons, only to return a childless widow. One of her two also-widowed daughters-in-law travels home with her, although she begs them both not to:

> *Return, my daughters. Why should you go with me? Have I yet sons in my womb, that they may be your husbands? Return, my daughters! Go, for I am too old to have a husband. If I said I have hope, if I should even have a husband tonight and also bear sons, would you therefore wait until they were grown? Would you therefore refrain from marrying? No, my daughters; for it is harder for me than for you, for the hand of the LORD has gone forth against me. (Ruth 1:11-13)*

When Naomi and Ruth arrive in Bethlehem, her old friends greet the pair with, "Is this Naomi?" She quickly tells them to call her not Naomi, which means "pleasant," but Mara, or "bitter," for, she says, "the Lord has witnessed against me and the Almighty has afflicted me" (verse 21).

Naomi was grieving her great loss. Openly and without shame.

Do you think, as I sometimes do, that if you allow the world to see your sorrow and regret over the losses you've suffered, you will ruin God's reputation? You will not. And neither will I. Honest grief does not indict God. To say that He is in control, even while you concede that bad things happen, is not to mar His character. If I trust Him with my life, I must trust Him with my grief.

I'm not issuing a cry-baby permit here. I'm saying that if you've suffered a real loss — the death of a spouse, a divorce you did not want, the babies you longed for but never had — God is well-equipped to handle your grief. He wants you to bring your tears to Him, and He doesn't require you to hide your sorrow from anyone else. He reserves the right to shape your future and offers the hope of redemption in the days to come. Just ask Naomi:

> So Boaz took Ruth, and she became his wife, and he went in to her. And the LORD enabled her to conceive, and she gave birth to a son. Then the women said to Naomi, "Blessed is the LORD who has not left you without a redeemer today, and may his name become famous in Israel. May he also be to you a restorer of life and a sustainer of your old age; for your daughter-in-law, who loves you and is better to you than seven sons, has given birth to him." Then Naomi took the child and laid him in her lap, [How sweet that must have been!] and [she] became his nurse. (Ruth 4:13-16)

Don't be afraid of your sorrow. Grieve if your heart is broken. But remember — God is not finished with your story quite yet.

For His anger is but for a moment, His favor is for a lifetime; weeping may last for the night, but a shout of joy comes in the morning.

(PSALM 30:5)

PERMISSION TO SERVE

Do you ever feel that because you are single, life owes you something? Not a mate, necessarily, but at least a *place*? Sometimes I think I have a right to fit in and feel comfortable. But do I really have that right? I'm not so sure anymore that comfort is my entitlement. But I am sure of this: Service is my call. Not my call because I'm single.

My call because I'm His.

I am called to imitate Christ — and Christ was a servant-king. He spoke quite clearly about His role: "Whoever wishes to become great among you shall be your servant; and whoever wishes to be first among you shall be slave of all. For even the Son of Man did not come to be served, but to serve, and to give His life as a ransom for many" (Mark 10:43-45).

Richard Halverson, former chaplain of the United States Senate, said:

> *Each day before I leave my study, I ask God to "wear me like a garment." My clothes are nothing in themselves — they are inanimate, and when I take them off they can't stand up or walk or do anything on their own. They collapse. I want to be like that in relation to Christ. I want my only animation to*

be Christ who lives in me, who thinks his thoughts, desires his
will, and loves his love through me.[10]

I want to want what Richard Halverson wanted, but sometimes I'm just selfish. Instead I want to be entertained. Or invited. Or pampered. Or pleased. I want to be considered first, and then spoiled a little. Even in my church, I want to have a place that suits me — and I often look for that place before I look to serve someone else.

I know too many singles who seem to be "on strike" until God delivers what they want. They're willing to serve — when they marry. But I wonder whether we'll be equipped to serve *in* marriage if we haven't managed to learn servanthood outside of it? A very successful single woman told me once, "I don't have time to do anything for God right now, but I give more money than a lot of people do." Ouch. I've never been in her shoes (I typically have more time than money, and not overwhelming amounts of either), although I understand that it's easiest to give what you have in abundance. But maybe what God desires most is that we learn to give out of our lack — depending on Him to multiply the gift and provide for the giver.

If we singles really imitated Jesus — if we really gave ourselves permission to serve — I believe the world would be changed. Or at least our small corner of it.

Is there a need you can supply? Is there a hurt you can soothe? Is there a word you can speak or a task you can shoulder? Paul challenged his brothers and sisters in Christ at Philippi to serve one another:

*Do not merely look out for your own personal interests, but
also for the interests of others. Have this attitude in yourselves which was also in Christ Jesus, who, although He
existed in the form of God, did not regard equality with God a
thing to be grasped, but emptied Himself, taking the form of a
bond-servant, and being made in the likeness of men.*
(Philippians 2:4-7)

Would you like to live like a king? My King took a towel and
washed His followers' feet. I want to imitate Him more than I
want to be liked. I want to follow Him more than I want to fit in.
And more than anything, I want to hear Him say to me, "Well
done, good and faithful servant."

---

*Therefore, since we receive a kingdom which cannot be
shaken, let us show gratitude, by which we may offer to
God an acceptable service with reverence and awe; for
our God is a consuming fire.*

(HEBREWS 12:28-29)

Perspective

Managing marriage expectations

*Are you so anxious for what is not yet yours that
you can't appreciate all that is? The secret is not to deny or
banish longing from our lives — or to allow it to
become our all-consuming idol — but to simply allow it
to exist along with our passion for life.*

WHAT DO YOU EXPECT?

"And they lived happily ever after." How often do *those* words appear at the end of some romantic story? The standard fairy-tale formula — boy meets girl, boy and girl fall in love, face insurmountable challenges, overcome those challenges, and wed — is neat, but woefully incomplete. Storytellers seldom speak of the days, weeks, months, and years that make up "happily ever after," and whether they really *are*.

Even real-life couples who struggle openly through courtship and engagement remain mostly mum about the gritty realities of married life. Whatever expectations they held before they said their vows get quietly (or not so quietly) put away, and husbands and wives get on with the routine business of living.

Singles are left to our own imaginations about the truth of one-flesh living and, with so little hard data to shape our ideas, we tend to fall back on the old stuff — the fairy tales. For that reason, our expectations may have little in common with real life. And that's too bad.

If you desire marriage, what do you expect it to deliver? An end to all loneliness? Financial security? Emotional intimacy? Constant companionship? Unending romance? Some expectations are so unrealistic that they virtually guarantee failure.

A friend of mine, who married for the first time in her forties, is frank about how little she knew of what marriage required. "I stood before him that day in church and thought I knew everything about him," she said. "We were two adults who had not rushed into marriage. We had dated for quite some time. We'd talked to each other about our plans and dreams. We thought we knew it all. But looking back, I can see that I had no real understanding of what it was I was promising. I didn't really know him — I barely knew myself! All I knew enough to say with any certainty on that day was, 'I promise not to quit.' The rest was a mystery to me."

My friend realized in retrospect that her wedding-day expectations had little basis in truth. But in the ensuing years, she has shaped an accurate view of what marriage can be. I believe she and her husband expected companionship. They expected a shared history, and they built it day by day. They expected laughter and tears, and have certainly experienced both. They expected the challenge of work, the comfort of shared beliefs, and the change that growth is sure to bring. They promised not to quit when they knew very little. They've kept that promise with fuller knowledge of one another, and they are keeping it still.

Marriage can be a great adventure, but a terrible idol. It can't deliver perfect love. It can't guarantee true peace or prosperity or security. Storing up years of unrealistic expectations and dumping them at the feet of an unsuspecting partner on the day "I do's" get said is hardly fair. Married or single, none of us knows what life will bring. Only God does. And only He can love us perfectly, bring us peace, and permanently and irrevocably secure our future — all reasonable expectations of the God of the universe.

For this reason I bow my knees before the Father, from whom every family in heaven and on earth derives its name, that He would grant you, according to the riches of His glory, to be strengthened with power through His Spirit in the inner man, so that Christ may dwell in your hearts through faith; and that you, being rooted and grounded in love, may be able to comprehend with all the saints what is the breadth and length and height and depth, and to know the love of Christ which surpasses knowledge, that you may be filled up to all the fullness of God.

(Ephesians 3:14-19)

GREENER GRASS

What gift are you hoping for, wishing for, longing for, right now? A mate? A date? A better job? A long vacation? Children? A financial windfall? Chances are your wishes, your longings, your desires, lie just beyond your ability to fulfill them. They may be just out of reach, but they're there — if you're honest enough to admit them.

Somewhere between childhood and adulthood we learn that it's safest to disguise our true desires, or at least to keep quiet about them. We learn to disregard the "greener grass" we yearn for, and focus instead on whatever satisfaction we *have* managed to find. We construct lives for ourselves where "busyness substitutes for meaning, efficiency substitutes for creativity and functional relationships substitute for love."[11]

We may willingly edit our desires, but God never asks us to. He knows what we may not yet understand: our desire — our longing for something more — can actually direct our hearts toward Him. In fact, Christianity has next to nothing to say to the person who feels completely happy with the way things are. Its message is for those of us who hunger and thirst.

Could it be that God is preparing you to receive more of Himself by frustrating you with *less* than you expected from life? Could the hunger in your heart today have less to do with the "greener grass" of marriage or a family or an exciting career than it does with a desire for a richer relationship with the living God?

Everybody tries to fill their "gaps" with something. Maybe you've tried to fill yours with religion, or work, or overeating, or too much shopping, or sex. Guess what? It won't work. Our restless hearts really were made to find their rest in Him. Nothing else completely satisfies. The comfort of any other fix is only temporary.

Are you ready to give up the dash for greener grass and follow your Maker "further up and further in"? You might be if . . .

• You're tired of performing to please others and dissatisfied with your accomplishments, even when others praise them.

• You don't appreciate the love you receive, but always seem to want more.

• You're bored with the things that money can buy, yet you still keep spending.

• You're longing for something more than you can get for yourself or the world can give.

Before God can open our eyes to the beauty of His Son, He must dim our satisfaction with the things of this world. Are you disappointed with what you have and are longing for more? Listen carefully. What seems like discontent could be the voice of your Beloved calling you closer to Him in love.

———

God, my desires fool me sometimes. I know the things I look longingly at from afar are not the things that will ensure my happiness. Help me to remember that in Your presence is fullness of joy, and in Your right hand there are indeed pleasures forever. The longings that I feel are not bad, but I need to follow them past the obvious and all the way back to their root. It really is You I want, You I need, You I thirst for, and You alone who can satisfy. Instead of searching for greener grass, help me lie down in green pastures and be satisfied in the company of my great, good Shepherd. I want my wants to be all wrapped up in You, Jesus. Guide me in the paths of righteousness for Your name's sake.

LISETTE'S WINDOW

Just a few blocks from my house on a tree-lined street stands a window I can't stop peering into. The window belongs to Lisette, and although she and I have never met, I've become familiar with her work.

Lisette is an artist who uses the medium of fabric and lace. She makes exquisite bridal gowns and displays them in the ground-floor window of the 1930s two-story that houses her studio. One stunning dress always appears front and center, facing the busy street, and I find it nearly impossible to drive past without ogling her newest design.

Lisette's window evokes two responses in my heart: awe at the sheer beauty of her lovely creations and a sharp longing that comes from being on the outside of this particular window, looking in. I'd like to go inside and touch the smooth satins and run my fingertips over the rich laces, but no one goes into a bridal salon "just looking." A wedding gown is not an impulse purchase. You don't shop for one until you need it, and up to now, I have not. I may be all grown up, but the elegant trappings of marriage remain just as elusive to me today as they were when I was seven or eight, staging pretend weddings with my dolls.

What does it feel like outside the marriage window, looking in?

It's humbling. It's humbling to still want something most people your age already have had at least once. And at times it's more than a little embarrassing to feel like an overgrown kid at the window of a candy store where all the sweetest confections remain just out of reach. But humility and occasional embarrassment are survivable. Clinging stubbornly to the belief that only marriage will complete or satisfy me — and that, unmarried, I will always be on the outside looking in — is not.

Missionary-in-training Jim Elliot wrote to his bride-to-be Elisabeth during a time of uncertainty and separation in their seven-year courtship: "Let not our longing slay our desire for living." Young Elliot left Wheaton College for South America to pursue a call to missions. He eventually married Elisabeth, but less than two years after they wed, wild tribesmen murdered him on the shores of an Ecuadorian river. Even in his too-short life, he managed to balance both a strong longing for marriage and a passion to live for Christ.

Are you on the "wrong side" of the window of longing? Are you so anxious for what is not yet yours that you can't appreciate all that *is*? The secret is not to deny or banish longing from our lives — or to allow it to become our all-consuming idol — but to simply allow it to exist *along with* our passion for life.

On a good day, I can appreciate the loveliness of the eye candy in Lisette's window without sighing deeply as I pass. On a good day, I can delight in all the other desires God has already fulfilled for me. After all, there *is* a wedding in my future. I'm certain of it. And I am already and always a beautiful bride to the One who has chosen for me what I will wear: the perfectly spotless and shimmering covering of His own righteousness that will fit as if it were my very own.

———————

I will rejoice greatly in the LORD, *my soul will exult in my God; for He has clothed me with garments of salvation, He has wrapped me with a robe of righteousness, as a bridegroom decks himself with a garland, and as a bride adorns herself with her jewels.*

(ISAIAH 61:10)

Let us rejoice and be glad and give the glory to Him, for the marriage of the Lamb has come and His bride has made herself ready.

(REVELATION 19:7)

Vulnerability

Letting yourself be known

The prerequisite for intimacy with another human being is
intimacy with God. Until we've experienced that, we're fooling ourselves
and each other. We're hiding or playacting or bluffing —
but we're not really experiencing loving intimacy. We can't be,
because we don't know how.

IS THAT A MASK
YOU'RE WEARING?

Plenty of good reasons exist to wear a mask. Divers wear them to breathe. Surgeons wear them for protection from germs. Welders wear masks to keep sparks of hot metal from burning their skin, and baseball catchers pull theirs tight to protect them from errant, 95-mile-an-hour fastballs. For these and others like them, masks are considered standard operating gear. They're essential to completing the job at hand.

Where masks aren't so useful is in our relationships with one another. There, they present more of a hindrance than a help. Singles — especially if we lack the accountability of a core group of intimate friends or family — may not only be quite adept at donning masks, but also more likely to get away with the deception they allow.

Relational masks guard against revelation, risk, or rejection. They can buy the wearer time to determine what "face" will offer the most advantage in any given situation. If you don't want to reveal too much, too soon, slip on the mask of agreeable compliance. You know the one: You pretend to enjoy baseball, fish tacos, or Bible study, because you're interested in someone who does — and you'll compliantly watch a game, dine at a taqueria, or delve into Paul's letter to the Galatians to prove it.

Afraid of being hurt? There's always the mask of mild disinterest, best worn with an air of nonchalance and heavily curbed enthusiasm, and accompanied by phrases like "I guess so," or "Sure, why not?" or "Whatever."

Also quite popular is the mask of spirituality. The wearer of this mask feigns an interest in spiritual things, promising a depth that eventually proves lacking. He or she may attend church, pray before meals, and quote Scripture liberally, but continued observation will reveal little "chinks" in the wearer's suit of religious armor.

We wear these (and other) masks mostly because we want to be accepted and loved. But mask-wearers eventually experience one of two results: Either they are found out and unmasked, and the relationship is damaged or irreparably broken; or their deception is *not* discovered, but their ensuing relationship is false, existing on a kind of emotional fault line that affords little joy and even less security.

Our propensity for "covering up" does not please God. Jesus confronted the "masked men" of His day, the Pharisees, with this strong rebuke: "You blind guides, who strain out a gnat and swallow a camel! Woe to you, scribes and Pharisees, hypocrites! For you clean the outside of the cup and of the dish, but inside they are full of robbery and self-indulgence" (Matthew 23:24-25). In Ephesians, Paul exhorts his friends to traffic only in the truth: "Therefore, laying aside falsehood, speak truth each one of you with his neighbor, for we are members of one another" (Ephesians 4:25).

The masks we wear to gain the world's approval prevent us from being truly known and loved. Everyone who's ever worn a mask has eventually discovered that love without real knowledge of the beloved is both cheap and unsatisfying.

Could understanding that we have *already* been seen, known, and perfectly loved by God in our "as-is" state make us brave enough to drop our pretenses once and for all?

———————

But God put his love on the line for us by offering his Son in sacrificial death while we were of no use whatever to him. Now that we are set right with God by means of this sacrificial death, the consummate blood sacrifice, there is no longer a question of being at odds with God in any way. If, when we were at our worst, we were put on friendly terms with God by the sacrificial death of his Son, now that we're at our best, just think of how our lives will expand and deepen by means of his resurrection life!

(ROMANS 5:8-10, MSG)

KEEPING IT REAL

An article in my local paper touted a new way to meet other singles: "the eight-minute date."

According to this article, the eight-minute dating phenomenon is catching on as a quick and painless way to screen would-be romantic partners. It works something like this: An eight-minute dating event gets promoted for a public gathering place. Interested singles come and are randomly matched with "dates" that last exactly eight minutes. During that time, they ask one another questions to gauge their "compatibility." At the end of eight minutes, a buzzer sounds and the process begins again with a new partner. Partners rate one another and, at the end of the evening, list which of their encounters piqued their interest enough to risk a second look. When both parties indicate a desire to meet again, notifications get sent out.

While I've had some dates that I *wished* could have ended after eight minutes, I'm not buying the eight-minute dating plan — and I'm not buying it for the same reason I waited ten years to purchase a microwave. I'm convinced that the quality of an end result relates directly to the time invested in the process. It's impossible to get a gourmet meal in less than five minutes — and it's impossible to know in eight minutes what sort of person you've just met.

Character and heart get revealed over time, in many kinds of situations. Two of my closest friends today would not be counted as cherished "inner circle" companions if we had based that decision on the first eight minutes of our meeting. One of them initially unnerved me with the sheer force of her megawatt, outgoing personality. I am much quieter in big gatherings and slower to warm up to strangers. The other walked into my living room, moved my furniture, and scolded my dog! Today, I love them both dearly — and my life would most certainly be poorer without them.

Anyone can "get real" for eight minutes, but "keeping it real" is a different story altogether. The temptation to believe that we can know another person in less time than it takes to choose a good melon might be strong — especially if we desire to avoid getting hurt or wasting precious time on something that might not work in the end. But the only way to know, really know, another is to make an investment of time and risk extended vulnerability.

My outgoing friend — the one who shines at parties — teaches high school students. Each year she reads to her seniors this passage from an eighty-year-old children's book:

> *"Real isn't how you are made," said the Skin Horse. "It's a thing that happens to you. When a child loves you for a long, long time, not just to play with, but REALLY loves you, then you become Real. It doesn't happen all at once . . . it takes a long time. That's why it doesn't often happen to people who break easily or have sharp edges or have to be carefully kept. Generally, by the time you are Real, most of your hair has*

been loved off, and your eyes drop out and you get loose in the joints and very shabby. But those things don't matter at all, because once you are Real you can't be ugly, except to the people who don't understand."[12]

My friend teaches what she knows. She's keeping it real.

How are you at "keeping it real"? Are you taking the time to know others and allowing them enough time to know you? Can you risk the vulnerability of revealing your "shabby" side even when you feel afraid? If you haven't tried before, what about starting today?

———

God, You know how frightened I can be of allowing others to see my heart. I wish it were stronger and sweeter and purer than I know it is. But I know, too, that iron sharpens iron, and that You can use the sparks that fly in that process to make me more of the person You mean for me to become. Help me to risk being vulnerable. Help me to commit to the time it takes to grow relationships of true value, so that the world will know Who I love by observing how I love.

LOVING THE HOLY ONE

Smarting from a recent breakup, I found myself talking through the relationship's demise with a newly married pastor and his wife. (I thought I was meeting only her for lunch, but she must have called in reinforcements; her husband arrived just behind us at the soup and salad spot, a place no man would likely pick on his own.) As we two women talked, our "third wheel" remained mostly silent. Then she looked at him and said, "Honey, what do you think?"

He put his fork down and looked me straight in the eye. "I think a man cannot be intimate with a woman until he has learned to be intimate with his God." Then he shrugged his shoulders, smiled kindly at me, and returned to his salad.

I don't remember one other thing spoken in that tiny restaurant by any of the three of us. Just those few words. And nearly five years later, I haven't forgotten them. I'm convinced they are true — and I'm convinced they are true not only for men.

The prerequisite for intimacy with another human being is intimacy with God. Until we've experienced that, we're fooling ourselves and each other. We're hiding or playacting or bluffing, but we're not really experiencing loving intimacy. We can't be, because we don't know how.

The word *intimacy* comes from the Latin word *intima*. It means inner, or innermost, and it implies being in touch with our inner selves. Most of us think of intimacy as a deep connection between two people, but before it becomes that, it is a baring of our true self. It's peeling the onion of our own heart, one paper-thin layer at a time. And we need God's help to do that. He alone can rightly reveal our inner man, then help us deal with what we see there.

King David must have remembered his own soul-baring experience before a holy God when he wrote Psalm 19:7-9:

> *The law of the LORD is perfect, restoring the soul; the testimony of the LORD is sure, making wise the simple. The precepts of the LORD are right, rejoicing the heart; the commandment of the LORD is pure, enlightening the eyes. The fear of the LORD is clean, enduring forever; the judgments of the LORD are true; they are righteous altogether.*

Spending time in God's presence and meditating on His Word caused David to look inward. "Acquit me of hidden faults," he wrote. "Also keep back your servant from presumptuous sins; let them not rule over me." When he saw the darkness in his own heart, he called on God to help him be a better man: "Let the words of my mouth and the meditation of my heart be acceptable in your sight, O LORD, my rock and my Redeemer" (verses 12-14).

Until we see our true self before God, we cannot bring that true self into any other relationship. Clinging to our false self while someone else clings to his or hers does not equal intimacy. And until we know that we are forgiven and loved by God as we are, we will always look for someone else to validate us.

An old friend of mine grew up in a small town in Louisiana. He had an expression for two people looking for something from one another that neither of them had to give. The first time I heard it, it made me wince. Then it made laugh. Then it made me think. *"Two ticks, no dog,"* he'd say knowingly. And without a strong, intimate, growing love relationship with our heavenly Father, that's what we are. We're feeders looking for a host, at the same time pretending to be "host material" ourselves.

There's only one source of unconditional love. There's only one source of truth. There's only one source for forgiveness and cleansing and wholeness. His name is Jesus. And until we know and are known by Him, we don't stand a chance for real intimacy with one another.

God — you're my God! I can't get enough of you! I've worked up such hunger and thirst for God, traveling across dry and weary deserts. So here I am in the place of worship, eyes open, drinking in your strength and glory. In your generous love I am really living at last! My lips brim praises like fountains. . . . If I'm sleepless at midnight, I spend the hours in grateful reflection. Because you've always stood up for me, I'm free to run and play. I hold on to you for dear life, and you hold me steady as a post.

(PSALM 63:1-3,6-8, MSG)

COMMUNITY

CULTIVATING INTERDEPENDENCE

Invest in the lives of those closest to you. Love those whom God has placed in your life right now — today. Don't think of their companionship as a consolation prize or a temporary substitute until the "real thing" comes along. They are the real thing.

COMMUNITY'S NOT "VIRTUAL"

Surf the Web for an evening and you'll discover "communities" of people you never knew existed. Iguana owners. Pilates enthusiasts. Parents without partners and partners without parents. Organic gardeners. *Andy Griffith Show* devotees. These and other like-minded folks connect in cyberspace and form virtual "communities," but most of them will never meet, never know one another's real names, and never share their stories offline.

So what kind of community is *that*?

Our technology-empowered culture works against the establishment of authentic community. Face it. If you live alone, it's far too easy to come home from work, lock the door behind you, click on the remote, turn on the microwave, let voice mail field your calls, and hold the world at bay. Anyone who wants to can readily become an island unto himself.

Even church is accessible from a distance. I can download sermons from my favorite teachers, access worship music from an MP3 file, and request prayer anonymously with an e-mail. (As far as I know, communion still remains a "virtual" impossibility.)

I'm not denouncing technology; in a very real sense, it pays my bills. But it's a poor substitute for the richness of a close, supportive, flesh-and-blood community of friends who know and are known by one another. Married or single, young or old, we are not made for isolation; we are made by God for *each other*. This is what He had in mind:

- Be devoted to one another in brotherly love; give preference to one another in honor; not lagging behind in diligence, fervent in spirit, serving the Lord; rejoicing in hope, persevering in tribulation, devoted to prayer, contributing to the needs of the saints, practicing hospitality. (Romans 12:10-13)

- . . . that there may be no division in the body, but that the members may have the same care for one another. And if one member suffers, all the members suffer with it; if one member is honored, all the members rejoice with it. Now you are Christ's body, and individually members of it. (1 Corinthians 12:25-27)

- Bear one another's burdens, and thereby fulfill the law of Christ. (Galatians 6:2)

Community doesn't just happen. We must seek it out. Maybe even go looking for it before it comes looking for us. If you feel detached, make that your cue to reach out to someone else. Don't e-mail or instant-message. Pick up the phone and call. Invite a friend out to dinner. Offer to run errands together. Plan a "mission of mercy" for a third friend who needs a lift. Instead of waiting for an invitation, extend one. And while you're doing whatever it is you've chosen to do together, talk. Not about the weather or other people, but about the things in your heart, and in his. Only the foolish wait to be in love to love.

A good friend I phoned once about a situation I could not control heard the note of panic in my voice. "Please pray," I pleaded.

"Let's do it right now," he replied. And he did. As I heard his words, I felt the sure and certain comfort of knowing I was not alone. And I made a mental note to do for someone else what he had just done for me.

Let us hold fast the confession of our hope without wavering, for He who promised is faithful; and let us consider how to stimulate one another to love and good deeds, not forsaking our own assembling together, as is the habit of some, but encouraging one another; and all the more as you see the day drawing near.

(HEBREWS 10:23-25)

NO WEDDINGS AND
THREE FUNERALS

I'm not the only unmarried woman in my circle of friends. In fact, three of my dearest friends, like me, have yet to marry. When I feel tempted to wallow in self-deprecating pity, I look at them and remember that a woman's marital status cannot possibly be a reflection of her beauty, or her worth. We four — an actor, an asset manager, a writer, and a teacher — have a delightful history that I would not exchange for any late-arriving knight on a white horse. (Although I certainly wouldn't send him packing.)

We have encouraged and supported each other through more years than any of us would like to admit and traveled delight and disaster shoulder-to-shoulder. Between us we've stood at the gravesides of two precious fathers and one long-suffering mother. We've been flung out of rafts and into whitewater together (literally!) and nursed each other's broken hearts with quiet compassion. We've questioned God out loud, but never doubted our shared faith. We've questioned each other, but never our good intentions. If *semper fi* was for girlfriends, we'd be Marines.

Quite simply, I cannot imagine my life without these friends. We've grown up together, and I'm blessed by that fact every day of my life. To me, they are a "close-up" of the beautiful body of Christ:

As a result, we are no longer to be children, tossed here and
there by waves and carried about by every wind of doctrine,
by the trickery of men, by craftiness in deceitful scheming; but
speaking the truth in love, we are to grow up in all aspects
into Him who is the head, even Christ, from whom the whole
body, being fitted and held together by what every joint sup-
plies, according to the proper working of each individual part,
causes the growth of the body for the building up of itself in
love. (Ephesians 4:14-16)

I am certain that if I had married at twenty-five, had children
by thirty, and settled quietly into the safety of the suburbs, I would
not have known that God could send His love in quite so many
tender ways, including through the faithfulness of lifelong friends.
Don't get me wrong; I still yearn for what I do not have. I want to
be married. I want to have children. My life's ambition was always
to be a wife/mother/writer. So far, I'm batting .333.

And I am more blessed than I ever could have dreamed.

Invest in the lives of those closest to you. Love those whom
God has placed in your life right now — today. Don't think of their
companionship as a consolation prize or a temporary substitute
until the "real thing" comes along. They *are* the real thing. And so
are you.

"And my God will supply all your needs according to His riches
in glory in Christ Jesus" (Philippians 4:19).

*Father God, thank You for never leaving me alone.
For providing companions for this odd and wonderful
journey that I never planned to take. Thank You for the
tears, both happy and sad, and for the triumphs we've
celebrated with one another. Thank You for the lessons
that my friends teach me, even when they're not trying.
They are the hands and feet of Christ to me when
Christ seems far away.*

*Teach me to celebrate every love, every friendship, every
consolation that You, in Your lovingkindness, bring to
me. Don't let me miss a single thing because I was looking for something else. You are good, and Your goodness
to me is everlasting. Don't let my discontented rants fool
You. I'm in excellent company, and I know it. Be it done
to me according to Your Word.*

EXTENDED FAMILY

The place I go most often for solitude — known colloquially as "the quiet house" — is tucked into the rolling landscape of the Texas hill country. It's so remote that I drive my car through a limestone riverbed to get there. In fact, my own car won't take me all the way. One of the foremen on the property must carry me the last quarter of a mile or so in a four-wheel drive vehicle and leave me utterly on my own until he returns to pick me up at a mutually agreed upon day and time.

The small, stone house has no phone, no television, no radio, and no clock. An hourglass sits on the ledge of the kitchen window seat, but nothing, save my own wristwatch, can put the individual hours into context. Even with no instruments or machines, the house has a rhythm, and the wind in the cedars plays its own music. Wood for a fire is laid in the fireplace, waiting to be lit, and fresh linens grace the bed.

The house provides a perfect setting for private retreat, but I am never entirely alone there. God's presence permeates the very air, of course — but there's more. I am, in my solitude, connected to a long line of pilgrims and saints who've come this way before me, and their company is both rich and real.

There are the men and women who lovingly conceived the place, and the ones who built it with their hands. There is the sweet woman I've never met who has taken my reservation by phone for several years and a groundskeeper who has carefully stacked extra firewood near the back door. I know that the houseguest before me swept the floor, hung fresh towels, and stripped and remade the bed, just as I will do for the unknown guest who'll follow me.

There are books in the bookshelf brought and kindly left by other travelers, and in the lower right-hand desk drawer a stack of stenographer's journals are filled with the thoughts and prayers of several years of sojourners. Although they contain the kinds of private things you might not tell a trusted friend, visitors are encouraged to read them. And so are they bidden to add secrets of their own. I have prayed over many of these, and I am sure that some have prayed for me.

I've never been to the quiet house with someone else — and yet I've never been there alone.

I've never been anything but single, either, and yet I can't say I've ever been entirely on my own. God in His great lovingkindness has supplied an extended family to surround me that, seen and unseen, has provided blessed company. The names of some of them sound familiar and dear to me, but others have remained nameless. From my third-grade Sunday school teacher to my two best friends from childhood, from my favorite love to the incredibly kind stranger who calmed my nerves on my first transatlantic flight — they are all gifts, each one. And they serve to remind me that I am never, ever completely disconnected or all alone. Quite the contrary!

I'm certain I have family I've yet to meet — and I look forward to making their acquaintance in God's good time.

Do you see what this means — all these pioneers who blazed the way, all these veterans cheering us on? It means we'd better get on with it. Strip down, start running — and never quit! No extra spiritual fat, no parasitic sins. Keep your eyes on Jesus, who both began and finished this race we're in. Study how he did it. Because he never lost sight of where he was headed — that exhilarating finish in and with God — he could put up with anything along the way: cross, shame, whatever. And now he's there, in the place of honor, right alongside God. When you find yourselves flagging in your faith, go over that story again, item by item, that long litany of hostility he plowed through.

That will shoot adrenaline into your souls!

(HEBREWS 12:1-3, MSG)

RELATING

LOVING THE ONES YOU'RE WITH

Each of us, married or single, needs community, shared histories,
and perspective. We need to be for one another the body of Christ,
both teaching and learning from each other,
regardless of our age or marital status.

WHEN FAMILY TIES
ARE TANGLED

Antone Quentin Fisher almost never made it to adulthood. He was born in prison to a crack-addicted mother who abandoned him; he spent the first two years of his life in an orphanage. The foster family who took him in repeatedly abused him, and a stint at reform school did nothing to heal his shattered heart. After living on the streets for a short time, he joined the U.S. Navy, and there he found the strength to search for his blood relatives and begin building a family of his own. Eventually, he decided to tell his story, and while working as a security guard on the Sony Pictures lot, he began the autobiographical screenplay called *Antwone Fisher*. Antone not only survived his past, he thrived in the unlikely wake of it.

For better or worse, most of what we know about relating to others and making our way in the world we learn from our family of origin. Perhaps you grew up in what was once viewed as the "typical" American family, with a father and mother and one or two siblings; but these days, there *is* no typical family. Single-parent homes are no longer exceptional, and stay-at-home moms are in the minority. Many children get reared by their grandparents or another relative. Some grow up in the care of foster parents or other caregivers.

Whatever the scenario, this much is certain: The home you grew up in shaped the person you became. Whether you are still living in that home or left it years ago, you still carry its imprint, as I carry the unique imprint of mine.

According to one clinical psychologist, the family is a primary, powerful influence on the relational patterns of our lives:

> Our family is like a classroom where we learn the skills and knowledge that will one day enable us to live outside it. Our families teach us to trust or distrust the people around us, to speak up or stay quiet in a social setting, to give or to take. They teach us what kinds of feelings are acceptable, appropriate and tolerable. Our family sets the pattern for all other relationships.[13]

If you grew up in a safe, loving, nurturing home, this is good news. If not, you probably have struggled well into adulthood. I have a friend who played the role of peacemaker during her childhood, and she often assumes that role in her own family and also in her job. Another friend grew up in a home where bad feelings either were not discussed or were quickly dismissed. Today, she finds it difficult to acknowledge when she feels hurt or sad or angry. Still another friend remembers growing up fatherless — knowing the identity of his dad, but never being acknowledged as his son. As a result he has struggled mightily with his identity.

LEIGH McLEROY | 133

Seeing, understanding, and dealing with your own family issues and oddities is difficult enough — but when you are in a relationship, you really are comingling your baggage with someone else's . . . and the result is rarely a nice, matching set of Samsonite!

It would be easy to despair of ever "getting it right" except for this: The Bible overflows with stories of what we would call dysfunctional families, yet God used them powerfully. He is a God of new beginnings. He changes us individually and from the inside out. And the one thing stronger and more powerful than the influence of our family of origin is His perfect love.

As adults, we have a responsibility for who we are today, regardless of our past. It is up to us to look back honestly, release those loved ones we may be holding hostage for old hurts, and recognize any negative or destructive patterns we have adopted without realizing it. If we need help, many, many resources are available.

God does not erase our past. He does even better than that. He redeems it!

Is there any "raw material" in your own history that cries out for His transforming touch?

I ask him to strengthen you by his Spirit — not a brute strength but a glorious inner strength — that Christ will live in you as you open the door and invite him in. And I ask him that with both feet planted firmly on love, you'll be able to take in with all Christians the extravagant dimensions of Christ's love. Reach out and experience the breadth! Test its length! Plumb the depths! Rise to the heights! Live full lives, full in the fullness of God.

(Ephesians 3:16-19, msg)

LOVING YOUR MARRIED FRIENDS

I'm no math whiz, but I retained enough of the basics to know that three is an odd number. When singles marry, their friendships change—and it takes effort to nurture an important friendship from a comfortable two to an accommodating three. I've learned that unless a friendship can stretch at least a little to include the friend's new mate, it isn't likely to survive past the newlywed years.

I've seen singles so jealous over a friend's marriage that it became hard for the friendship to continue. I've also witnessed the occasional clash between friends and fiancés. (Friends usually lose.) But when our friends marry well, those of us who remain single are blessed. We not only gain another friend, we gain the side of our old friend that only his or her mate calls forth. We see a new facet of a person we thought we knew inside out.

The majority of the friends I made in my early single years are married now. Most of them have children. We don't see each other as frequently as we did in less encumbered days, and when we do, we often feel rushed and distracted. The most important thing is that we make the effort to connect, because relating to someone in a different stage of life enriches us incredibly. My life would be decidedly monochromatic without my married friends, older friends, friends who are a decade or so younger, and the children I know and love. If I spent time only with other singles, my view of the world would be skewed.

As a single woman, I can lapse into the belief that I have little to offer my married friends — but I know that is a lie. Each of us, married or single, needs community, shared histories, and perspective. We need to be for one another the body of Christ, both teaching and learning from each other, regardless of our age or marital status.

I'm still surprised when my sister calls me with a parenting challenge, since we both know I have no children. What she does know is that I love her and her family, and that even without real-life experience, I have a perspective that might be helpful.

Singles are not silly. Singles are not irresponsible or shallow or "less than" in any way. Singles are simply unmarried. That's all. So what I bring to my married friends is me — unmarried. I bring to them what I bring to any friendship: my gifts, my heart, my passions, my sense of humor, my insight, my words, and my way of seeing the world. In addition, I can and should bring to our friendship these things that my single status affords me.

A *slightly idealized view of marriage*. When married friends struggle with the challenges of living "yoked" to someone else, I believe it helps to hear from one who thinks that their sometimes cumbersome and complicated arrangement is a thing to be desired and valued. Nothing raises the stock of what you have more than realizing that someone else wants it.

A *living example that the grass is not always greener*. Everyone, at some point, thinks he or she is on the wrong side of the fence. By being honest about my struggles as a single person, I allow my married friends to remember that freedom had its disadvantages too.

Unselfish encouragement. There are times when singles do not support or seem enthusiastic about the dating relationships of our fellow single friends. We can be overly critical or jealous or simply consumed with our own issues. But if we are not "competing" with them in any way, it's easier to be unselfish about supporting, encouraging, and nurturing someone else's relationship.

An uncompelled love for their children. I can remember adults who loved me in my childhood years simply because they could. They weren't relatives or teachers or "professionals" in any way. Many times they were friends of my parents, and I delighted in their interest in me and the fact that they weren't required in any way to offer it.

My prayers. I need to pray not just for my married friends, but for my married friends' marriages. That they would be strengthened and encouraged by one another. That their love would grow. That their homes would become places of safety and peace and empowering love.

Bear one another's burdens, and thereby
fulfill the law of Christ.

(Galatians 6:2)

LOVING FRIENDS OF THE OPPOSITE SEX

"The differences between a man and a woman," said G. K. Chesterton, "are at best so obstinate and exasperating that they practically cannot be got over unless there is an atmosphere of exaggerated tenderness and mutual interest."[14] Although Chesterton wrote these words nearly a century ago, you'll get no argument from me on their present-day validity. Men are different. (And men — I know — we are too!)

Not only are we different but those differences are *good*.

One of the biggest challenges we singles face is how to rightly love the opposite sex outside of the established framework of marriage. It's a challenge to love not one man or one woman, but men and women in general. To love not a husband or a wife, but our opposite-sex friends.

While I grew up in a mostly girl family, early on I came to my appreciation of men. I adored my dad as a little girl and would go anywhere with him just for the pleasure of his company. If he picked up the car keys, I was "in." It could be a trip to the hardware store, the gas station, or the city dump, and I was scrambling for the passenger seat. We must have shot thousands of free throws from our back patio while I was growing up. His presence was the contrasting difference in our all-girl house, and I appreciated it. I still do.

My earliest childhood friends included some boys too. I liked the forts they built and the rough-and-tumble, competitive games they played, even though they weren't so keen on dolls or stuffed animals. High school and college brought male friends as well. We looked out for one another, commiserated when one of us suffered a breakup, and cheered each other's accomplishments.

I like men not in spite of our differences, but because we're different. It is precisely this other-ness that I appreciate in my male friends. They see situations, challenges, and even other people in ways counter-intuitive to me. They confound me and challenge my thinking. The best male-female friendships I've experienced seem to thrive when neither of us has (or develops) a more than passing romantic interest in the other. But the balance in opposite-sex friendships is fragile. Sometimes feelings change.

In response to the age-old question, "Can men and women be friends?" C. S. Lewis wrote, "In most societies at most periods friendships will be between men and men or between women and women. The sexes will have met one another in affection and in eros, but not in this love. For they will seldom have had with each other the companionship in common activities which is the matrix of friendship." But, Lewis said, when a man and woman "discover that they are on the same secret road . . . the friendship which arises between them will very easily pass — may pass in the first half-hour — into erotic love. Indeed, unless they are physically repulsive to each other or unless one or both already loves elsewhere, it is almost certain to do so sooner or later."[15]

So, *can* a man and a woman be friends? I think the answer is yes, for a season. Can it be longer than that? I believe it can, if they are never attracted to one another, or if they are — and they marry each other!

How can we best love our opposite-sex friends? Carefully. Respectfully. And honestly, so that if feelings change, they get acknowledged and dealt with.

Is it worth the special care it takes to maintain friends of the opposite sex? Absolutely. Together, we are made in the image of God. "God created man in His own image, in the image of God He created him; male and female He created them" (Genesis 1:27).

To see the world through only feminine eyes is to see it in half-light. To see it through only masculine eyes is the same. We are designed to complement one another, and we do. That is something God Himself pronounced "very good."

———

God, thank You for those challenging, confounding,
delightful others that enrich my life and reflect Your
image back to me. Make me appreciate what they bring to
my life and respectful of our differences. Keep me honest

in my dealings with them and honest before You, always. And God, if there is one man in particular You'd like me to pay closer heed to, lead me there, then help me to respond to his lead. Now, and then — I'm following You.

DATING AND RELATING

I never, ever meant to become a dating expert. But the truth is I've spent two-thirds of my life in dating-mode. Given the fact that I'm still single, maybe it would be more accurate to say that I've become a dating *veteran* rather than an expert. Either way, I have far more experience than I ever hoped to acquire in the peculiar process of the relational trial and error we call dating. I would like to report that it gets easier with practice.

I'd like to, but I can't.

These days, it's hard to find two people who even agree on what constitutes a date. Do group activities count? Is it about who asks, or who pays? For those of us who haven't kissed the whole dating process goodbye, what are the rules? Is it possible to ascribe to "biblical dating" if no one in the Bible dated at all?

I don't have the answers. I wish I did. But if I read these words from Proverbs correctly, the way men and women relate to one another romantically always has been more mystery than science: "There are three or four things I cannot understand: How eagles fly so high or snakes crawl on rocks, how ships sail the ocean or people fall in love" (Proverbs 30:18-19, CEV). It's almost as if wise old Solomon scratched his head and said, "You got me. Go figure."

Whether you've been burned one too many times in a dating

relationship or you're just plain burned out on the process, here are a few things to bear in mind.

There are far worse things than spending a Saturday night in your own company. The world will not end if one or many weekends go by without a date. A friend once told me that a woman confided to her, "If I knew right now I would never be married, I'd want to die." She wasn't kidding, either. Surely we have more to live for than *that*.

Men are specially created to initiate. Things seem to work much better when they do. Nothing feels nicer for a woman than to be given a straightforward and unambiguous invitation.

Women are specially created to respond. The temptation to manipulate and maneuver gets the better of us at times, but in our dealings with men, I believe we're most satisfied when we're "returning serve."

You date a person. A whole person. Not a face, a balance sheet, an image, or a title. A real, flesh-and-blood person who is made in the likeness of Almighty God. Your date is someone created with eternity in mind and who is completely unique. Respect that. Even better, honor it.

Your dating habits speak. Mine do too. We should take care what they say, not only about us, but about our God. Are you honest? Kind? Considerate? Does the way you conduct your romantic life stand in stark contrast to what the rest of the world considers the norm?

Courtship is a complicated dance, no doubt about it. Sometimes language fails us, like it did young King Henry in Shakespeare's *Henry V*. The British boy-king defeated the French army at Agincourt, and, along with France, won the hand of the

French princess, Katherine. He spoke to her (in English) and tried to woo her even though she was already his by treaty. She responded (in French) with hesitation. When his pleadings failed to bring the answer he sought, he became all man and all business. He put forth his hand to clasp hers, and said, "What say you lady? Clap hands and a bargain," then sealed the deal with a stolen kiss.

It's never that easy, is it? So we keep meeting people and making dates, hoping to learn how it is that people fall in love. And even when we're weary of it, we keep trying — because the process is every bit as important as the hoped-for end result.

Now for this very reason also, applying all diligence, in your faith supply moral excellence, and in your moral excellence, knowledge, and in your knowledge, self-control, and in your self-control, perseverance, and in your perseverance, godliness, and in your godliness, brotherly kindness, and in your brotherly kindness, love. For if these qualities are yours and are increasing, they render you neither useless nor unfruitful in the true knowledge of our Lord Jesus Christ.

(2 Peter 1:5-8)

SELF-CONTROL

SAYING "YES" TO SAYING "NO"

*I don't know one person who has reached adulthood without
wishing for at least one major "do-over." But we can't revise history
or deny that its events have had a major impact on our lives.
What we can do is allow God to redeem our past — all of it — by
giving us not simply a new resolve, but a complete rebirth.*

EVERYONE'S *NOT*

Every now and again I suspect that I am the only unmarried person in America who is not having sex. It's not hard to see how such a perception might develop, since sex quite literally saturates our popular culture. From the movies to "reality" entertainment shows to music, literature, and advertising, sex is front and center. It certainly *seems* like everyone is "doing it." I *know* that everyone's not. But statistically speaking, the majority seem to be.

The vast majority of teenagers today have sex before their twentieth birthday. In the late 1950s, 46 percent of nineteen-year-old women were sexually experienced; in the mid 1980s nearly 70 percent were. Fewer than 20 percent of nineteen-year-olds of *either* sex were virgins by the late 1990s. With adolescents maturing earlier and young adults marrying later, it is estimated that most men and women are now sexually active for eight or more years before they wed. That's *if* they marry. More than three million single adults now live together as what the U.S. Census Bureau terms "unmarried partners with a close, personal relationship."

So my feeling that I'm in the minority (although not entirely alone) is well founded. It's considered more odd today to be an unmarried, celibate person than to move from sexual partner to sexual partner with no thought of a permanent, lifelong commitment.

"Free sex" used to be countercultural. Now freely chosen celibacy seems a more radical lifestyle.

Please don't misunderstand. I'm not saying I'm never tempted. I'm not saying it has been a breeze thus far. But I am saying that it's possible to love deeply and not fall into bed — and I know it from experience. I know that everyone's *not*— and I know because *I'm* not.

How is that possible? I can offer two reasons.

First, because I truly believe I've been given a gift. Sexuality is a God-given and beautifully wrapped "present" that can be opened for the first time only once. I prefer to savor this gift at the right time, under the right circumstances, because I believe what its Giver has said about its worth.

Second, I'm absolutely certain I am loved. If there were a serious love deficit in my life, the temptation to fill it with sex would almost certainly feel overwhelming. But the relationship that I have with Christ can fill my deepest longings for love and intimacy *if* I will allow it to and *as much* as I will allow it to. My choice to reserve sex for its intended home of marriage has much more to do with love and desire than it does with obedience and dread.

When I was a child, I had relatives in West Texas who farmed. Each harvest season, they hired extra workers to bring in their crops of cotton and maize, and to work in the cotton gin that they owned. One year, my aunt took the waist and inseam measurement of every single worker and bought each one a new pair of jeans, wrapping the packages up in bright paper and ribbons and handing them out to each man.

Every gift was the same. Blue jeans. No surprises there. But when the gifts were distributed, one man did not open his. He could see what his package contained, and he wanted the contents. But his box remained in his lap — taped, tied, and perfectly wrapped. When others encouraged him to open it, he said no, he would rather keep it as it was. It was a pretty package, he said, and he'd never had his own wrapped package. He would wait until he was ready to wear the jeans, and he felt happy to do so.

My sexuality is God's gift to me. He has allowed me to hold it. I can choose to open and enjoy it right now, or I can wait. Wrapped, it is lovely. I'm sure that unwrapped it will be even lovelier. With the help of His empowering grace, I'm going to wait until the time is right. Even though I'm aware that everyone else is not.

That means you must not give sin a vote in the way you conduct your lives. Don't give it the time of day. Don't even run little errands that are connected with that old way of life. Throw yourselves wholeheartedly and full-time — remember, you've been raised from the dead! — into God's way of doing things. Sin can't tell you how to live. After all, you're not living under that old tyranny any longer. You're living in the freedom of God.

(ROMANS 6:12-14, MSG)

TEMPTATION AND TRANSPARENCY

Most of us singles have more than a passing acquaintance with sexual temptation. We know what it's like to struggle with sin. And that temptation will not simply go away. None of us will wake up one bright morning and say, "Boy, those urges to sin are gone! I no longer want what is not mine, and I'm not tempted to satisfy my body at the expense of my soul." It just doesn't happen.

Martin Luther quipped that, while we are not able to stop birds from flying around our heads, we *can* stop them from building nests in our hair. In other words, the extent of the damage done by temptation, to a great degree, depends upon us. "Nests" are built — and real damage done — when temptation turns to lust.

Lust exists where our desires are our masters, rather than our servants. Lust is placing primary importance on a secondary thing — any secondary thing. The trouble is it's very hard to know exactly when we are about to become servants to what we should master or when we are beginning to place primary importance on a secondary thing. There's no hard-and-fast line. It would be easier if there were.

The question many single Christians ask is, "How far is too far?" We want to know where, along the continuum of desire, we can comfortably camp without falling into sin. Only, where sexual temptation is concerned, hardly anyone is comfortable to remain in the same place, are they? We want to press a little more, inch forward a little farther, and dare one another with another touch, another minute, or another halfhearted "no."

Then a funny thing happens. When physical intimacies that have no place in dating or courtship creep in, real communication begins to wane. That's because it's easier to touch or tease or kiss than it is to talk. It's easier to default to the physical than to do the hard work of getting to know another person's mind and heart.

The greatest temptation we face, however, is not the temptation to "get naked." It's the temptation to not get naked *enough*. One writer explained it this way: "Many couples trade the growth of long-term intimacy for short-term physical pleasure, sabotaging any chance they may have at real knowledge and commitment."[16]

Physical intimacy without emotional intimacy provides little lasting satisfaction. The "knowing" that comes with sexual intercourse is meaningless apart from being known emotionally and spiritually as well. That's the sort of knowing we should be most concerned with as singles. Now is not the time for physical nakedness with one another. Now is the time for us to explore one another's hearts and souls if we believe we are in a relationship that could lead to marriage. The transparency we begin to build on this side of marriage will set the stage for the total transparency that will come on the other side.

Sex outside of marriage is not something to be prized, no matter how gratifying it may seem. "It has more in common with a sneeze than a symphony," writes Ed Young. "It bears less resemblance to the transcendent than does a Harlequin romance novel. Premarital sex is about as far from real intimacy as a flea circus is from a safari. So, instead of thinking of what you may be missing . . . think of what you could be gaining by saying yes to a higher love."[17]

God, don't let me cheat in this critical area. When temptation hits hard, I may need to run instead of rationalize. Give me the courage to talk when it would be easier not to. Convict me when I say something with my eyes or with a touch that I would not say with my words. I want to deal in truth. And I want to build a foundation for a strong, open, honest marriage, if marriage is in my future. Keep me transparent before others, and most importantly, before You. I want to please and honor You, Father, in all that I do.

STARTING OVER

"Born Again Virgins." That was the title of the article in a popular women's magazine — and I have to admit, it caught my attention. When I read it, I learned that a "born-again virgin" is someone who has *not* abstained from sex in the past, but has decided to place an embargo on the act until_____ (fill in the blank).

Some of the article's subjects felt determined to wait for the one they deemed Mr. or Ms. Right before having intercourse again. Others simply had grown tired of casual sex or were concerned about contracting a sexually transmitted disease. A few were engaged and/or living together and believed that postponing sexual intimacy with their current partner until *after* the ceremony would enhance their future physical relationship. Whatever their reason, these "nontechnical" virgins had decided to try on abstinence again, and many found it to their liking.

At least two things struck me as I read. One, that while the term "born again" in a spiritual context usually gets derided in mainstream media, it has somehow become cool — even cutting edge — to say you're "born again" in a sexual sense. Two, that each of us has a past, and within it, things we might like to revise. Maybe they are sexual things, or maybe they're words that we'd like to take back, or roads that we'd like to have detoured. I don't know a single person who has reached adulthood without wishing for at least one major "do-over," including me. But we can't revise history or deny that its events have had a profound impact on our lives when they have. What we can do is allow God to redeem our past — all of it — by giving us not simply a new resolve, but a complete rebirth. He doesn't redeem just one tiny section of our lives. He wants the whole thing.

C. S. Lewis said it this way:

> Christ says, "Give me all. I don't want so much of your time and so much of your money and so much of your work: I want You. I have not come to torment your natural self, but to kill it. No half-measures are any good. I don't want to cut off a branch here and a branch there, I want to have the whole tree down. Hand over the whole natural self, all the desires which you think innocent as well as the ones you think wicked — the whole outfit. I will give you a new self instead. In fact, I will give Myself: My own shall become yours."[18]

Do you want to be made completely new? That's His best offer. In fact, that's His *only* offer. No partial refurbishing or revisionist history. *Newness.* And not a newness that denies your past, but one that sees it, embraces it, and co-opts it completely for your good and His glory.

The scribes and the Pharisees brought a woman caught in adultery, and having set her in the center of the court, they said to Him, "Teacher, this woman has been caught in adultery, in the very act. Now in the Law Moses commanded us to stone such women; what then do You say?" They were saying this, testing Him, so that they might have grounds for accusing Him. But Jesus stooped down and with His finger wrote on the ground. But when they persisted in asking Him, He straightened up, and said to them, "He who is without sin among you, let him be the first to throw a stone at her."

Again He stooped down and wrote on the ground. When they heard it, they began to go out one by one, beginning with the older ones, and He was left alone, and the woman, where she was, in the center of the court. Straightening up, Jesus said to her, "Woman, where are they? Did no one condemn you?" She said, "No one, Lord." And Jesus said, "I do not condemn you, either. Go. From now on sin no more."

(JOHN 8:3-11)

COURAGE

MAKING THE DECISION TO LOVE

You may not have heirs in the traditional sense. I don't.
You may not have a fortune to bestow or a legacy
of great works that will outlive your fleeting days on
this planet. But if you're brave enough, you can
leave a "love trail" that will linger long after you've gone.

THE VIEW FROM 13,000 FEET

The occasion: one of those birthdays that end in zero. Five of my friends arrived to pick me up at the appointed hour, and I had with me the things they'd said I would need: jeans, tennis shoes, a sweatshirt, heels, pantyhose, a nice dress, and my swimsuit (in January?). I had no idea where we were going, but they looked jazzed. We chattered in the car for more than thirty miles, then turned off the interstate into the middle of nowhere. I saw a few metal buildings in the distance, then the sign: *Municipal Airport*, and in smaller letters, *Home of Skydive USA.*

I felt thrilled for two reasons. First, I'd always said there were two things I wanted to do before this particular birthday, and skydiving was definitely one of them. Second, I felt relieved *not* to don my swimsuit, tanless, in the dead of winter. My birthday gift from these girlfriends was a tandem parachute jump from three miles up, connected in all the right places to my many-times married, multiple-tattooed, body-pierced jump instructor, Tom. (Despite how little we had in common, we bonded in less than sixty seconds.)

After viewing a video introduction, receiving one-on-one training, donning my gear, and signing the scariest waiver I've ever seen, I was set. Our small, noisy prop plane climbed to the required height, and Tom and I commando-crept forward. With my face to the open doorway and Tom at my back, we rocked gently twice, and on the third forward motion, we fell into the sky. Only one thought came to mind before the cold air hit my face and took my breath away: *I've been here before.*

No, I'd never skydived before, but the faith-and-falling feeling was nothing new. I felt it on my first day of school, at my first dance recital, in the seconds just before my first kiss, and at the instant I placed my eight-year-old heart in the hands of Jesus. It came again as my parents drove away from my freshmen dorm, hit hard on my first real job interview, and still happens every time I stand before an audience to speak.

That feeling has taught me that courage isn't the absence of fear, but the simple presence of faith in the face of it.

Are you afraid? Living life solo can feel scary. Will there be enough money to pay the bills? Will love ever come and stay? Will my children be all right or will I fail them somehow? Will I grow old all alone? Lose my job? Will my tests come back with good results or will the news sound grim? Will my secret past be discovered or my worst failures brought to light?

No one can say.

But when you're braced at the door of your own particular risk *de jour*, looking down from 13,000 feet, the best advice I can give is this: Breathe deeply. Appreciate the view. And when the moment comes to trust, rock gently forward into the thrilling free-fall of faith. You'll be okay — Someone's got your back.

_____

"No man will be able to stand before you all the days of
your life. Just as I have been with Moses, I will be with
you; I will not fail you or forsake you. Be strong and
courageous, for you shall give this people possession of the
land which I swore to their fathers to give them. . . .
Have I not commanded you? Be strong and courageous!
Do not tremble or be dismayed, for the LORD your God
is with you wherever you go."

(JOSHUA 1:5-6,9)

And without faith it is impossible to please Him, for he
who comes to God must believe that He is and that He is
a rewarder of those who seek Him.

(HEBREWS 11:6)

RISKY BUSINESS

"Of all the arguments against love," wrote C. S. Lewis, "none makes so strong an appeal to my nature as 'Careful! This might lead you to suffering.'" Lewis readily admitted his own preference for what he called "safe investments and limited liabilities," but he also saw the danger of nurturing a steadfastly cautious heart: "The only place outside Heaven where you can be perfectly safe from all the dangers and perturbations of love," he wrote, "is Hell."[19]

Not much of a choice, is it?

I haven't been divorced, but I have friends who have. I haven't lost a mate to death, but I know many who have endured that tragedy. Once you've loved deeply and lost, no matter how, you're undeniably vulnerable. To love again is no assignment for the weak or timid. Loving with abandon requires courage, but it is a risk well worth taking. "Go after a life of love as if your life depended on it," wrote the apostle Paul, "because it does" (1 Corinthians 14:1, MSG).

The Bible abounds with courageous characters who went after love when it would have been easier to retreat. There is Mary, the unwed teenage mother of God-in-the-flesh, who greeted the angel Gabriel's stunning announcement of her pregnancy with these fearless words: "Behold, the bondslave of the Lord; may it be done to me according to your word" (Luke 1:38). Not only was the timing terrifyingly wrong for her to have a baby, she was called to bear and love a child who would never really be her own in the way other mothers' children were. (One modern woman of unfaith declared, "If I had been the Virgin Mary, I would have said 'No.'")[20]

Then there is Ruth the Moabitess, who lost her husband, then forsook her homeland to travel with her also-widowed mother-in-law to a land she'd never seen. There, in Israel, she became both a foreigner and a beggar, yet she boldly invited the love of a good man who took her as his wife. God blessed their unlikely union with a child, and she became grafted into the lineage of Christ Himself.

Perhaps the courageous lover whose story most inspires and amazes me is a man named Abraham. At the direction of God, he took his long-awaited son, Isaac, up to a high place on Mount Moriah, and there planned to put him to death. Abraham loved his son. He didn't understand why God would ask such a thing of him. But he obeyed. "Then they came to the place of which God had told him; and Abraham built the altar there and arranged the wood, and bound his son Isaac and laid him on the altar, on top of the wood. Abraham stretched out his hand and took the knife to slay his son" (Genesis 22:9-10).

Isaac did not die. After Abraham had raised his hand with the knife, an angel of God appeared and told him: "Do not stretch out your hand against the lad, and do nothing to him; for now I know that you fear God, since you have not withheld your son, your only son, from Me" (verse 12). When Abraham looked around, he saw a ram caught in the thicket nearby and offered it up instead on the altar he had built for his son. Can you imagine it?

This kind of courageous, beyond-human-limits love in the face of loss *is* possible — but only when we know that we are loved beyond all limits by God Himself. He is the One who gives us the courage to risk our hearts and love with abandon and obedience. And we can be sure we are loved in just this way because God did for us what He did not, in the end, require of Abraham. He sacrificed His only beloved Son on our behalf.

Love is not safe — but God has loved us anyway. Will you risk loving as you have been loved?

Beloved, let us love one another, for love is from God;
and everyone who loves is born of God and knows God.
The one who does not love does not know God, for God
is love. . . . In this is love, not that we loved God,
but that He loved us and sent His Son to be the
propitiation for our sins. Beloved, if God so loved us,
we also ought to love one another.

(1 JOHN 4:7-8,10-11)

THE COURAGE TO LEAVE
THINGS BEHIND

I've always been intrigued by epitaphs, small handfuls of words meant to capture the essence of a life. Some are sweet: "Beloved wife and mother." Others are brief and to the point: "Here lies _____." Some are greeting-card poetic: "As the flowers are made sweeter by the sunshine and the dew, this old world is made brighter by the likes of folks like you." A friend of mine once suggested that my epitaph should read, "Finally... I'm fine," because of my frequent insistence, no matter what the circumstances, that I really am "just fine," thanks.

I have stood near the graves of my own loved ones and others the world knew but I did not — Winston Churchill, Napoleon, C. S. Lewis, J.R.R. Tolkien, Clare of Assisi — and wondered, *How do you sum up a life? Who chooses the closing words?*

The "who," of course, are others. And they get their material from observing how we live. They form their remembrances from the stuff we leave behind. Only, not the stuff we leave behind at the end, because most of us have no idea when the end will actually arrive. It's the stuff we leave behind in every conversation, every meeting, every celebration, every task, every touch, and every trial.

A few years ago, I sat in a crowded sanctuary with others who had gathered to honor my good friend, Charlie. He died at forty-seven. He never married. He served Jesus all his life. Not perfectly, but simply. Consistently. Faithfully. A large screen was suspended high above the pulpit, and on it appeared his name and the calendar dates that comprised the bookends of his brief but lovely earthly life.

Ordained men delivered eulogies. Those blessed with lovely voices sang — and so did less-gifted friends like me, in chorus with the gathered congregation and the host assembled higher above us. In his death, Charlie ushered us into worship, because in his life, Charlie ushered us into worship. It was the bright red thread woven through his days, and he left it behind. He didn't leave children. He didn't leave a fortune. He didn't leave a great magnum opus that generations will revere. He left that part of himself that he treasured most. And he left it everywhere.

At his very sickest, after an outing with a small group of friends that must have felt like climbing Everest, Charlie called and spoke these words to me: "I hope that you can see that I'm okay . . . in fact, I'm getting better. Underneath it all, Leigh, I'm getting better." He was dying, and we both knew it. And yet, he had the courage to show his friends not only his broken body, but his unbroken spirit. He *was* getting better. I could see it. And I told him so. For just an instant, I saw the unseen glory of the Resurrection. And it was Charlie who showed it to me.

You may not have heirs in the traditional sense. I don't. You may not have a fortune to bestow or a legacy of great works that will outlive your fleeting days on this planet. But if you're brave enough, you can leave a "love trail" that will linger long after you've gone. The sum of your life — of mine — will be nothing more and nothing less than what we dare to leave behind.

God, teach me to consider my legacy, even as a family of one. Open my heart and let Your love flow through me, with the distinctive scent of sacrifice and the powerful wind of praise. I'm not rich. I'm not well known. Sometimes I feel completely insignificant, but I see only the temporal, while You see the eternal. Let me leave my best stuff behind like Charlie did. I am richer because he dared to live and love in response to Your heartbeat. Help me live so that others can feel the weight of Your glory when I'm gone.

JOY

REFUSING TO BECOME BITTER

Joy is tricky. It's elusive. It can't be mustered or summoned, nor can it be canned and kept. It is a by-product of my relationship with God that, more often than not, catches me off guard.

When Will I Have Joy?

My alarm did not go off. I had no time to wash and dry my hair, virtually ensuring a frightful hair day. I'd put off getting gas the evening before, and now, because I was running late, I had no choice but to risk fate and hit the freeway with the needle already past "E." I had an 8:30 A.M. meeting (what was I thinking?) and a day that left me room to do little more than breathe in and out until after 5:00 P.M.

And to top it all off, I was out of coffee.

Then on the way to work (praying for the fumes to deliver me), I saw the bumper sticker that put the icing on my lopsided cake: "No Jesus, no joy. Know Jesus, know joy."

I felt braced for a "no joy" day, based on the way mine had begun. As I made my way through traffic, I mentally composed my own self-styled bumper sticker: "No one to wake me up if the alarm fails to ring, no joy." Or, "No one to fill up my car when I'm too busy, no joy." I even toyed with "No one to deliver me from this miserable existence, or at least work hard so I can stay home and join the Junior League, no joy." (Too long, I decided.)

In my heart of hearts, I know the truth of the bumper sticker's message. But I'm also tempted to think that at least a *little* bit of joy might be found elsewhere. Especially in the things that my life lacks.

Aren't you?

There's just one problem. If I can't seem to locate joy now, what guarantee do I have that a mate or a family or someone to share life's responsibilities with will change that? And if I had those things, then lost them, would I lose joy as well?

Joy, I'm discovering, is tricky. It's elusive. It can't be mustered or summoned, nor can it be canned and kept. It is a by-product of my relationship with God that, more often than not, catches me off guard. And while I believe that finding a life partner will be a joy-ful thing, I don't (except on really rotten mornings) think it will bring me unconditional joy, or everlasting joy. Only the things that last forever can bring us lasting joy. Jesus lasts forever. And because I've placed my faith in Him, so will my joy.

A year or so ago I hosted a baby shower in my home. Two dear friends had adopted a son from Russia, and we wanted to celebrate his arrival. It was the third shower I'd given in a matter of months. As I prepared for my guests, I began counting in my mind the baby showers and bridal showers I had either hosted or attended that year. I reminded God that at none of them was I the guest of honor. (I'm sure this was not news to Him.) I did not feel happy about the flood of chattering women I'd invited to descend on my living room, although I had well prepared myself to hide the fact.

Then my friend and her new son arrived, and her mother and mother-in-law. What an adorable little boy! The doorbell rang again and two more friends I hadn't seen in a very long time entered. Hugs all around. Soon the room filled, and we laughed and passed the baby from lap to lap, celebrating how good God had been to bring him from such a very long way at just the right time.

Oddly enough, in the midst of everything, I forgot I felt miserable. Not only that, somehow, along with all the other guests who'd gathered, joy entered unannounced. And I had let him in.

When will I have joy? Maybe when I stop trying to be the one who decides "when," and choose to simply leave the door ajar.

You will make known to me the path of life; in
Your presence is fullness of joy; in Your right hand
there are pleasures forever.

(PSALM 16:11)

SIMULTANEOUS CONTRAST

It was one of the oddest songs I'd ever heard at a funeral, but the leader asked everyone present to sing. So we stood to our feet and sang the words to a gospel hymn called "Be Ye Glad." Here's an even odder thing: Even through my tears, I *was* glad. Not that my friend had gone. Not that death had taken him from us. But glad that, in this case, death did not have the last word, only a brief pause in a long and lovely tale of grace.

We'd come to mourn, but instead we sang. We felt both brokenhearted at our own loss, and thrilled at the triumph of Jesus' victory over death. And a deep gladness — unexpected but solid — permeated everything. Death could not snuff out joy; it only spotlighted it, like a shining diamond on a black velvet cloth.

An artist friend would have called it "simultaneous contrast."

Simultaneous contrast describes the ability of the eye to change the appearance of color shades depending on the surrounding colors. That means an artist doesn't really know the true value of a color when he squeezes it from its tube or places it on his palette. It becomes apparent only by the influence of the surrounding colors once it's applied to the desired spot on the canvas. Somehow, the eye provides a kind of contrast, intensifying color differences and making them more recognizable.

"Straight from the tube," we might not even recognize joy. But in the stark contrast of suffering, we perceive it more clearly. Most of us, of course, would prefer to receive our joy straight. We don't want the clarity that comes from contrast. We want peace and ease and warmth and fuzzy comfort.

We don't want loneliness. We don't want fear. We don't want worry or loss or broken hearts. But without them, we just might miss joy.

"For His anger is but for a moment," wrote King David, "His favor is for a lifetime; weeping may last for the night, but a shout of joy comes in the morning" (Psalm 30:5). Joy comes in the morning. And the morning comes after the night. There's more. "Those who sow in tears shall reap with joyful shouting" (Psalm 126:5). First tears, then joy. Jesus explained it this way: "Therefore you too have grief now; but I will see you again, and your heart will rejoice, and no one will take your joy away from you" (John 16:22). Yes, there will be sorrow. But with it, joy. "Joy," said G. K. Chesterton, "is the gigantic secret of the Christian."[21]

Do you hurt? Are you mourning for someone or something that isn't? Don't despair. We often find the deepest joy in the context of suffering. It seems improbable, but it's true. Consider the "simultaneous contrast" of your present circumstances and be on the lookout for that mysterious thing called joy.

_____

God, I am so quick to indict You when my circumstances seem hard or sorrowful. I should know by now that hard times are Your cue, and that You are never far from the stage in any scene of my life. Teach me to anticipate Your unheralded entrances and to relish the contrast that shows You for the kind of God You are: One who loves me far too much to leave me alone in my despair, and also too much to remove it entirely. I want to see Your goodness and feel Your joy. Use whatever means You see fit to illuminate them both.

LOVING SMALL DELIGHTS

We three grown women piled into a back booth at a local diner, terrorizing our not-yet-legal waitperson with ridiculous requests, ordering food we could have eaten with impunity at seventeen, and laughing like we *were* seventeen. We have known each other since we were kids, but hadn't seen one another in several years. We had more catching up to do than we could have possibly covered in one night.

We've come a long way from the summer we all worked together at a local drugstore, where we spent most of our time trying on nail polish and looking at other people's photographs. Now we're the kind of people we used to take orders from: a school teacher, a stay-at-home mom, and a single "career" woman.

My two best friends from high school still look the same to me more than twenty years after our graduation — except they're both married and the mothers of double-digit-aged children. When we talked about our lives, I felt right at home, grounded again by their familiar voices and mannerisms. I even managed to ignore the nagging feeling that I had underachieved in the mate and procreate categories, until one of them asked the question I knew had to come: "So, are you seeing anybody?"

Suddenly I didn't feel grown up anymore. I felt sixteen and awkward. (Only, when I was sixteen and awkward, I *was* seeing someone.) I said, "No, not right now." And I felt the joy that had welled up when I saw my friends seep out of me like air from a pricked balloon.

I know it shouldn't be that way. I know I should count my blessings. But considering two of the blessings I lack — a husband and children — can numb me in an instant to the myriad of small gifts that overflow my life. "Hope deferred makes the heart sick," wrote Solomon the king, "but desire fulfilled is a tree of life" (Proverbs 13:12). I understand. I cherish a hope that, for now anyway, has been deferred. Sometimes my heart feels sick about it. In my admittedly flawed personal interpretation of the Bible, I took this verse to mean that the things I want but don't have make me sick and sad, but when I finally get them, I will feel glad and nourished.

Thankfully, my not-so-comforting self-translation misses the mark. I've discovered that the two words used here, "hope" and "desire," are not interchangeable. "Hope" is an expectation. And "hope deferred" is an expectation that is drawn out, extended, or delayed. Any strong expectation that has not yet materialized can make your heart ache. No surprise there. "Desire," on the other hand, is no long-held expectation, but a delight, a satisfaction, or a dainty charm. When that small delight arrives, Solomon said, it arrives like a sweet savor.

The trouble comes when my delayed expectation dulls my capacity to savor the sweet, small delights that already are mine in abundance.

For the record: As of yet, no husband. No children. Expectation delayed.

Also for the record: A short list of delights that *are* mine (and they are only a sample):

• Dinner with two precious, lifelong friends.

• A cute but spoiled fifteen-pound ball of canine fur that curls up in the crook of my arm while I'm reading, licks my wrist, and sighs.

• The eighteen-year-old with a mountain of troubles who called this year to wish me happy Mother's Day. (Even though I'm not his mom.)

• Lunch with the two most adorable nieces on the planet.

• Holding a good friend's hours-old son while watching A&M beat OU on television (a double-dose of delight!).

• Hearing my best friend pray out loud for me.

• Crafting an almost-perfect poem.

• Attending matins in the lower chapel of the Basilica of St. Francis, surrounded by Giotto's amazing frescoes (another sensory double-whammy).

• The perfect half-moon outside my window tonight.

Hope deferred can threaten to crowd out my joy and make my heart sick. But oh, those small delights — they are sweet food for a hungry heart, and precious, every one.

How long, O LORD? Will You forget me forever? How long will You hide Your face from me? . . . But I have

trusted in Your lovingkindness; my heart shall rejoice in
Your salvation. I will sing to the LORD, *because He has*
dealt bountifully with me.

(PSALM 13:1,5-6)

PRESENCE

DRAWING NEAR TO GOD

What if a change of focus could produce a change of heart,
and a change of heart could produce a new life?
Would you be interested? What if there was something so
wonderful, so beautiful, so glorious to behold
that you'd never be able to reach the end of it,
even if you had forever to try? There is.

PRESENT IN LONELINESS

I suspect one of the great joys of marriage will be the continuing *presence* of one who is like you, yet wholly different. My married friends endorse my view — yet they also quickly point out that the near-constant proximity of another human being is one of the great *challenges* of married life.

Do you imagine that a mate might satisfy the hunger we singles feel for that "otherness"? The truth is, none of us at *any* stage of life is immune to loneliness.

We feel lonely when we are isolated not by choice but by circumstances that seem beyond our control, when we feel disconnected, unseen, undervalued, or unloved. Sometimes the presence of others can keep those negative feelings at bay, but they can just as easily arise in a room full of friends or at a quiet, romantic table for two. Other human beings, even ones we dearly love, can never completely fill our longing for the constant, comforting presence of another. But a great gift lies hidden in the vacancy of loneliness that seldom gets experienced so clearly anywhere else.

Loneliness is a place where God comes in and makes *His* presence known.

Consider Hagar, a lonely single mother and the slave of Abraham's wife, Sarah. She became a pawn in Sarah's frustrated attempts to "help" God fulfill His promise of a son.

> *So Sarai said to Abram, "Now, behold, the LORD has pre-vented me from bearing children. Please go in to my maid; perhaps I will obtain children through her." And Abram lis-tened to the voice of Sarai. . . . He went in to Hagar, and she conceived; and when she saw that she had conceived, her mis-tress was despised in her sight. (Genesis 16:2,4)*

What never looked like a good idea quickly became untenable. The relationship between Sarah and Hagar broke down. Sarah despised both Hagar and her son, Ishamael. The feelings were mutual.

Sarah and Abraham eventually had a son of their own, Isaac, and the situation between the two women became even worse. One morning Hagar found herself banished with nothing but a loaf of bread and a skin of water. She and Ishmael were left utterly alone. When their water ran out, Hagar put her son in the shade of a bush and sat down near enough to hear him, but not to see him die. Both of them wept aloud. And then, without warning, they discovered another Presence with them in the wild:

> *God heard the lad crying; and the angel of God called to Hagar from heaven and said to her, "What is the matter with you, Hagar? Do not fear, for God has heard the voice of the lad*

where he is. Arise, lift up the lad, and hold him by the hand, for
I will make a great nation of him." (Genesis 21:17-18)

When Hagar opened her eyes, she saw a well of water she had not seen before. She filled her skin with it, gave her son a drink, and began a new life with him.

In her loneliness, Hagar was never alone. I'm sure she felt desperate and abandoned, but God knew exactly where she was. He heard her there. When she came to the end of her courage and her resources, she heard His voice. And when she followed His instruction, she saw provision that she had not previously noticed, although she could not have been far from it.

In the wilderness of our despair, God's presence becomes most obvious. It may seem that you sit all by yourself in your lonely place — but you do not. Comfort — the powerful, permanent presence of God Himself — is closer than you ever dared to hope.

Sing to God, sing praises to His name; lift up a song for
Him who rides through the deserts, whose name is the
LORD, and exult before Him. A father of the fatherless and
a judge for the widows, is God in His holy habitation. God
makes a home for the lonely; He leads out the prisoners into
prosperity, only the rebellious dwell in a parched land.

(PSALM 68:4-6)

PRESENT IN STRESS

"If you come out of the raft," our female river guide instructed, "float downstream on your bottom with your feet out in front of you." Two friends and I had planned a whitewater rafting trip down the Arkansas River, and we were listening to last minute how-to's as we strapped on our life jackets. "Then what?" one of us asked.

"Someone will pick you up," she said. "When they hold out their oar, grab on, then they'll pull you over the side." By then we had already seated ourselves in our big rubber raft, which we had no intention of leaving under any circumstances. The river ran fast. And cold.

The first part of the excursion, the smooth part, enabled us to carry on a conversation. Our guide — one of those early-twenties, very tan, less-than-10-percent body fat adrenalin lovers — had been working the river for years. She knew what she was doing. So when she stopped mid-conversation and began barking out orders in a drill sergeant's voice, we obeyed. But apparently not quickly enough to maneuver safely through something called "Satan's sinkhole." Within thirty seconds of the first 360 degree spin, all three of her passengers flew into the water; we popped out like ping-pong balls, one after the other.

"Feet out!" she screamed. "Float down!" (Like we had any choice.) Once I could see again, I did as she said, fixing my eyes on the toes of my sneakers, looking around for another raft, and trying to locate my friends. I don't know how long I stayed in the water, but I remained (I discovered the next day) long enough to acquire some pretty wicked bruises.

Soon a raft full of strangers paddled close, extended an oar, and pulled me alongside. Someone grabbed me by the shoulders of my lifejacket and very ungracefully hauled me over, dropping me face down in the bottom of their craft. (My first thought: *Thank goodness I'll never see these people again*, quickly followed by, *Thank you, Jesus*.) In a matter of minutes, separate rafts safely rescued all three of us. And so we made the remainder of our journey downstream.

The next day, we decided that the out-of-the-raft part of our trip had been the highlight! It felt plenty stressful while it was happening, but we'll never forget the incredible feeling of bobbing along in the strong current of a wild river. And our rescue made the memory sweeter still.

Living single can seem like a breezy river trip. It can feel delightful, and the scenery looks breathtaking at times. It can also seem a lot like getting tossed into a fast, freezing river with no help in sight. A layoff feels terrifying with no backup income. Illness is a threatening thing to face on your own. Decisions about children would be easier to manage with a sounding board, but often we don't have one. Caring for aging parents on your own presents a special kind of challenge.

"Life's hard," a good friend of mine likes to say, "but God's good." He is, indeed. And He is present in our stressful, scary times. He never abandons us when trouble comes.

How do I know this? Experience. And that's the point. You have to hit the river to know He'll take you through it. Peaceful floating trips are nice, but it's the rapids, sinkholes, and hairpin curves that convince us we do not ride alone. I think that must be why never-married Paul could, without regret, catalog his hardships:

> [I've been] beaten by Roman rods three times, pummeled with rocks once. I've been shipwrecked three times, and immersed in the open sea for a night and a day. In hard traveling year in and year out, I've had to ford rivers, fend off robbers, struggle with friends, struggle with foes. I've been at risk in the city, at risk in the country, endangered by desert sun and sea storm, and betrayed by those I thought were my brothers. I've known drudgery and hard labor, many a long and lonely night without sleep, many a missed meal, blasted by the cold, naked to the weather. (2 Corinthians 11:25-27, MSG)

Then he firmly declares:

> Now I take limitations in stride, and with good cheer, these limitations that cut me down to size — abuse, accidents, opposition, bad breaks. I just let Christ take over! And so the weaker I get, the stronger I become. (2 Corinthians 12:10, MSG)

We have no guarantee we won't land in life's river at some point along the journey; more than likely, we will. But when we do, we learn the truth we most need to know: It's the River-maker who carries us home.

God, I don't thrive on stress, but I do thrive on Your presence in every circumstance. Use the times that are a little scary and wild to remind me that You are all-powerful, all-wise, and all-sufficient. You are the One I want riding to my rescue, because I completely depend on You. I trust You to pull me out of whatever river I'm in, and then gently remind me what I learned while I was there.

PRESENT IN WORSHIP

Can you name the most underdiagnosed malady of single adults today? It's "me-itis." (I know. I've been exposed, but hopefully, I am not a carrier.) Without the competing needs of a significant other and/or children, many of us fall into the trap of believing it's all about us.

It's not.

The quickest way to misery is to live for self. The surest road to emptiness is to seek our own desires. Jesus said,

> *"Anyone who intends to come with me has to let me lead. You're not in the driver's seat — I am. Don't run from suffering; embrace it. Follow me and I'll show you how. Self-help is no help at all. Self-sacrifice is the way, my way, to finding yourself, your true self. What good would it do to get everything you want and lose you, the real you?"* (Luke 9:23-25, MSG)

It seems strange that the way to joy should come through denial, that the way to save our lives is to let them go. Human nature sees self-steering as best. Our instincts argue that it's up to us to get what we need and make the most of what we have. That's why so many of us feel unhappy and dissatisfied. We've been listening to ourselves.

What if a change of focus could produce a change of heart, and a change of heart could produce a new life? Would you be interested? What if there was something so wonderful, so beautiful, so glorious to behold that you'd never be able to reach the end of it, even if you had forever to try?

There is.

Someone has said that the good news of the gospel of Christ is that we are far more wretched and desperate and wicked than we ever dared to imagine — and that we are more completely loved and cherished by God than we ever hoped to dream. In a world where our own decisions seem terminal and our own destinies seem fixed, it is possible to begin again and be made new.

When a man named Nicodemus (married or single? Who knows?) met Jesus, the Son of God, he knew he had encountered something new. He complimented Jesus on the signs and miracles He'd done, and said, "No one can do these signs that you do unless God is with him" (John 3:2). So close to the truth, but still light years away! God wasn't "with" Jesus; He *was* Jesus. The living God Himself stood before Nicodemus. Jesus was God in the flesh.

Then Jesus told Nicodemus something that sounded strange to his ears. "Truly, truly I say to you, unless one is born again he cannot see the kingdom of God" (verse 3). Nicodemus, a grown man, didn't see how he could be born again — and he said so. Jesus answered,

"Unless one is born of water and the Spirit he cannot enter into the kingdom of God. That which is born of the flesh is flesh, and that which is born of the Spirit is spirit. Do not be amazed that I said to you, 'You must be born again.' The wind blows where it wishes and you hear the sound of it, but do not know where it comes from and where it is going; so is everyone who is born of the Spirit." (John 3:5-8)

Nicodemus didn't see how these things could be. Jesus told him that his problem had to do with his eyesight; he was trying to see the things of heaven with earthly eyes. "If I told you earthly things and you do not believe, how shall you believe if I tell you heavenly things?" (verse 12). Then, in a different time and a different place, in a different language to a different man, Jesus spoke the words that brought life to me nearly two thousand years later:

For God so loved the world, that He gave His only begotten Son, that whoever believes in Him shall not perish, but have eternal life. For God did not send the Son into the world to judge the world, but that the world might be saved through Him. (John 3:16-17)

Jesus saved me, once upon a time. He saved me from my sin. And He saves me every day of my life from myself. Without Him, I would believe it was all about me. (How could I not?) But by His grace, I am free to see that it really is all about Him. About His worthiness. His love. His power and presence and peace.

I worship Him not only when I attend church or pray or teach, but when my love for Him overflows my sense of self and permeates every corner of my heart and life. And in that holy place of wonder and awe, I am never, ever alone.

And neither are you.

The thief comes only to steal and kill and destroy; I came
that they may have life, and have it abundantly.

(JOHN 10:10)

1. Roland H. Bainton, *Here I Stand* (New York: Penguin Books, 1995), p. 225.

2. Lewis Smedes, *Forgive and Forget* (San Francisco, Calif.: HarperSanFrancisco, Reprint edition, 1996), p. 5.

3. Smedes, p. 84.

4. Oswald Chambers, *My Utmost for His Highest* (Updated Edition) (Grand Rapids, Mich.: Discovery House, 1995, 1992 by the Oswald Chambers Publications Association, Ltd.), January 13.

5. C. S. Lewis, *The Four Loves* (London: Geoffrey Bles, London, 1960), p. 139.

6. Charles Spurgeon, *12 Sermons on Prayer* (Grand Rapids, Mich.: Baker, 1980), p. 56.

7. Nancy Guthrie, *Holding On to Hope* (Wheaton, Ill.: Tyndale, 2002), p. 87.

8. Dr. Seuss, *Oh, the Places You'll Go* (New York: Random House, 1990).

9. Chambers, January 6.

10. Bruce Barton, Ron Beers, James Galvin, LaVonne Neff, Linda Taylor, David Veerman, eds., *Practical Christianity* (Wheaton, Ill.: Tyndale, 1987), p. 59.

11. Brent Curtis and John Eldredge, *The Sacred Romance* (Nashville: Thomas Nelson, 1997), p. 6.

12. Margery Williams Bianco, *The Velveteen Rabbit* (New York: Doubleday Reissue edition, 1958), p. 5.

13. Les and Leslie Parrott, *Relationships* (Grand Rapids, Mich.: Zondervan, 1998), p. 43.

14. G. K. Chesterton, "The Equality of Sexlessness," editorial, *G.K.'s Weekly* (July 26, 1930).

15. C. S. Lewis, *The Four Loves* (London: Geoffrey Bles, London, 1960), p. 79.

16. Ed Young, *Pure Sex* (Sisters, Ore.: Multnomah, 1997), p. 132.

17. Young, p. 138.

18. C. S. Lewis, *Mere Christianity* (First Touchstone Edition, 1996), p. 169.

19. C. S. Lewis, *The Four Loves* (London: Geoffrey Bles, London, 1960), p. 139.

20. Stevie Smith in *The Portable Curmudgeon Redux*, ed. Jon Winokur (New York: Dutton, 1992), p. 312.

21. George Sweeting, *Great Quotes and Illustrations* (Dallas: Word, 1985), p. 155.

About the Author

Leigh McLeroy is a contributing writer of seven books, including *Romancing the Home* and *Everywhere I Go*. A graduate of Texas A&M University, Leigh worked as an on-camera news reporter before venturing into advertising and marketing. She speaks to groups across the country and has led many Sunday school and home Bible studies for singles. A self-described "not-yet-married-but-still-quite-hopeful" person, Leigh makes her home in Houston, Texas.

Private Moments

Private Moments

Private Moments

Private Moments

Private Moments

Private Moments

Private Moments

Private Moments

Private Moments

Other books in the
New Life Live! Meditations series.

Moments for Couples Who Long for Children

With encouraging stories and helpful advice, Ginger Garrett, who has battled infertility herself, gently leads couples to a new sense of hope in God's compassion.
by Ginger Garrett
1-57683-472-7

Moments for Families with Prodigals

How can you help your son or daughter who has wandered from God? This book helps you claim scriptural promises and shows how you can participate in God's work in your prodigal's life.
by Robert J. Morgan
1-57683-473-5

To get your copies, visit your local bookstore, call 1-800-366-7788, or log on to www.navpress.com. Ask for a FREE catalog of NavPress products. Offer BPA.

NAVPRESS
BRINGING TRUTH TO LIFE
www.navpress.com

New Life Live! Meditations